BEYOND THE CROSS

Alfred Prempeh-Dapaah

Copyright © 2018 by Alfred Prempeh-Dapaah.

All rights reserved. No part of this publication may be reproduced, distributed, or transmitted in any form or by any means, including photocopying, recording, or other electronic or mechanical methods, without the prior written permission of the author, except in the case of brief quotations embodied in critical reviews and certain other noncommercial uses permitted by copyright law.

Except otherwise stated, all scripture is taken from the King James Version of the Holy Bible (Public Domain)

Printed in the United States of America

ISBN: Paperback: 978-1-948172-92-9
        eBook: 978-1-948172-91-2

Library of Congress Control Number: 2018948759

Stonewall Press
363 Paladium Court
Owings Mills, MD 21117
www.stonewallpress.com
1-888-334-0980

Contents

CHAPTER ONE: THE CROSS OF CHRIST 1
   The Power of The Cross 1
   Self-denial 9
   Persecution, Affliction and Suffering 19
   Mockery 26
   Crucifixion to the Old, Dead and Fallen Nature 30
   Suffering and Pain in the flesh 33
   Humiliation, Rejection and Loneliness 36
   Divine Reconciliation and Peace 38
   God's manifested Love 43
   The nature of God's love 50

CHAPTER TWO: BEFORE THE CROSS 57
   Christ Jesus knew where he came from 59
   Christ Jesus knew who he was . . , , , , , ... 61
   Christ Jesus knew why he came 64
   Learning from the Master 68
   Christ Jesus knew where he was going 73
   Christ Jesus lived in constant communion with the Father . . . 74
   The Master's Prayer life 75

CHAPTER THREE: POSITION OF THE CROSS OF CHRIST 81

- At the Cross 87
- The Kingdom of God 92
- Identifying with the Cross 94
- Identity before the cross 95
- CHAPTER FOUR 101
- NO MORE ON THE CROSS 101
- Neither is he anymore in the tomb 105
- He is risen from the dead and ascended into heaven 105
- And alive forever more 106
- Our great High Priest 107
- Our great Intercessor 108
- The Shepherd and Bishop of our souls 109
- Our soon coming King 110
- No one knows when 111
- But how ready are you 112

CHAPTER FIVE: LOOKING UNTO JESUS 113

- Where I am 116

CHAPTER SIX: BEYOND THE CROSS 121

- In conclusion 127

CHAPTER ONE

THE CROSS OF CHRIST

••••••••••••••••••••

> For Christ sent me not to baptize
> But to preach the gospel; Not with wisdom of words,
> Lest the cross of Christ Should be made of none effect
> For the preaching of the cross is to them that
> Perish foolishness; but unto us which are
> Saved it is the power of God
> 1 Corinthians 1:17-18

THE POWER OF THE CROSS

THE CROSS OF CHRIST which sometimes is referred to as the cross of Calvary because of the crucifixion which took place there, is revealed in the bible as the power of God. It is the power of God for the salvation, the redemption and the total deliverance of all mankind. There in that place called Calvary, our Lord Jesus Christ was crucified to die on the cross. In that place the only begotten and the only beloved Son of God was made to hang on the cross. He was made to suffer and bled to death as a curse for mankind so that mankind will be free from all the curses of life. The bible declares;

> Christ hath redeemed us from the curse of the law,
> Being made a curse for us: for it is written,
> Cursed is every one that hangeth on a tree:
> Galatians 3:13

Yes, in that place the Son of God was crucified, sacrificed on the cross as the propitiation for the sins of the whole world. We read from the epistle of John;

> And he is the propitiation for our sins:
> And not for ours only, but also for the sins of
> The whole world
> 1John 2:2

> Herein is love, not that we loved God,
> But that he loved us, and sent his Son to be
> The propitiation for our sins
> 1John 4:10

And yes, on the cross at the place call Calvary, the Son of the living God, Jesus Christ the Messiah was made to die as the sacrificial Lamb of God to take away the sins of the whole world. John the Baptist on two occasions declared to confirm this concerning Jesus Christ as the Lamb of God while he was in this world and walked on the face of the earth.

> The next day John seeth Jesus coming
> Unto him, and saith, Behold the Lamb of God,
> Which taketh away the sin of the world
> John 1:29

> Again the next day after John stood,
> And two of his disciples; and looking upon Jesus
> As he walked, he saith, Behold the Lamb of God!
> And the two disciples heard him speak,
> And they followed Jesus.
> John 1:35-37

And the bible records that the cross of Christ is the power of God unto us that are saved and believe; why? Because on that cross, the powerful saving miracle of God to redeem mankind was not only made manifest; it was also demonstrated through its works by the death and the shed blood of Christ. Christ Jesus died that we may be saved, have life and have it more abundantly. He shed his blood that we might be redeemed.

> For as much as ye know that ye were
> Not redeemed with corruptible things, as silver
> And gold, from your vain conversation received by
> Tradition from your fathers; But with the precious Blood of Christ,
> As of a lamb without blemish and without spot: Who verily was
> Foreordained before the foundation of the world but
> Was manifest in these last times for you,
> 1Peter 1:18-20

Now, the power of the cross of Calvary and for that matter the cross of Christ does not lie in the crucifixion per say. The power of the cross of Calvary lies in the personality of Jesus Christ who was crucified and made to hang on it. Crucifixion was already a sort of death penalty in the Roman era and thousands of criminals had already died through crucifixion even before Jesus Christ was born. It was a sign of criminal death or death by curse as the bible says; cursed is every one that hanged on a tree (Galatians 3:13).

However, the cross has become popular to represent the crucifixion by the death of Jesus Christ on it that all over the world, it has become a popular logo for the Christian faith. And though there might be different interpretation to the cross; wherever the cross is seen, the first likely thought that comes in mind is the crucifixion of Christ and something that has to do with the Christian faith. So after thousands of years the significance of the cross still continues; and that reveals the sign of its continued power through which many have come to be redeemed, saved, delivered, healed and made whole.

It is the power of God unto us that are born again by the incorruptible word of God (1 Peter 1:23); and unto us that are born of his Spirit (John 3:6). Oh yes, it is the power of God for and unto us that are in the Spirit (Romans 8:9), live in the Spirit and walk in the Spirit (Galatians 5:25; Romans 8:1, 4) and are led by the Spirit of God

(Romans 8:14). This is all because, it takes a divine encounter with the cross of Christ to experience this power of God that redeems, saves, delivers, heals and makes whole.

In another place when the apostle Paul went preaching to the Corinthians, he said to them that he would not want to know anything but to declare the testimony of God concerning his only begotten and beloved Son Jesus Christ and he alone crucified. It was on the cross that Christ got crucified. His crucifixion on the cross of Calvary gave power to the cross. And by talking about Jesus Christ and only him crucified, the apostle Paul also revealed how that God through the cross manifested and brought about his redeeming and saving power unto mankind. The power of God through the cross is also demonstrated by the raising up of Jesus Christ from his death on the cross; a resurrection that also gives hope of resurrection for them that would also believe in Jesus Christ.

Thus in a way, the cross becomes the power of God unto salvation and redemption to whoever believes in Jesus Christ. The apostle Paul said to the Corinthian church;

> And I, brethren, when I came to you
> Came not with the excellency of speech or of wisdom
> Declaring unto you the testimony of God
> For I determined not to know anything among you
> Save Jesus Christ and him crucified
> And I was with you in weakness, and in fear
> And in much trembling and my speech and my preaching
> Was not with enticing words of man's wisdom
> But in demonstration of the Spirit and of power
> That your faith should not stand in the wisdom of men
> But in the power of God
> 1 Corinthians 2:1-5

If the cross is the power of God then our faith in the power of God is also our faith in the cross of Christ. Here, the apostle Paul indicates for us to put our faith in the cross, perhaps not the cross as just a common piece of wood joined and put together for the crucifixion. Neither do we have to put our faith in the cross because Jesus Christ died on it. Rather, we put our faith in the cross as the power of God based on the personality of Christ Jesus who was purposely sent by God the Father to be crucified; and the activities of what actually took place with him involved on the cross. This also involves the things that happened around him on the cross to reveal God's intentions in relations to his plan of salvation for mankind.

So therefore, as we call into memory the cross of Jesus Christ or the cross of Calvary, our attention should be more on the person who hung on it and the activities that went on around him to bring about the fulfillment of God's plan for man's salvation. This means that in the eyes of the Father, it was a must that His only begotten and his only beloved Son suffers and die by the means of the cross in order to save mankind. It could not have been in any other way as it was confirmed in the prayer of our Lord in the garden of Gethsemane. The bible records it this way;

> He went away again the second time,
> And prayed, saying, O my Father, if this cup may
> Not pass away from me, except I drink it,
> Thy will be done.
> Matthew 26:42

You see, God's plan to save mankind through the cross of Christ Jesus is that which actually gives importance to it. This plan of God had to do with all and everything that took place with him even before he came into this world and went to the cross; his heading towards his crucifixion with the cross on his back to the moment he was crucified and made to hang on the cross to die the painful death. Not only that but also the activities on the cross and after the cross. These are the things that place worthiness on the cross for us to believe in its power. These also cause us to take glory in the cross of Christ without being ashamed as the apostle Paul again reveals when he said;

> But God forbid that I should glory
> Save in the cross of our Lord Jesus Christ
> By whom the world is crucified unto me
> And I unto the world
> Galatians 6:14

The cross as the power of God unto us is that which causes us to be crucified unto the world in Christ when we come to believe and trust in him with all our hearts. In a sense, we are spiritually crucified and made dead with Christ in a way that by the cross of Christ, the world with its cares and lusts of other things are crucified unto us. And we are also crucified unto the world with its cares and lusts of other things. In this case those things no more have dominion over us in Christ (Mark 4:19; Luke 21:34-36).

Crucified and made dead unto the world with the world dead unto us, we are in this world but not of this world. Neither should we be conformed to the world. In his prayer to the Father concerning his people on earth and in this world, Jesus said;

> I have given them thy word; and the world hath hated them,
> Because they are not of the world, even as I am not of the world
> I pray not that thou shouldest take them out of the world,
> But that thou shouldest keep them from the evil
> They are not of the world, Even as I am not of the world
> John 17:14-16

And the Lord assures us with these encouraging words;
> These things I have spoken unto you,
> That in me ye might have peace
> In the world ye shall have tribulation:
> But be of good cheer; I have overcome the world.
> John 16:33

Then the Apostle Paul also encouraged us as to how by his words;
> And be not conformed to this world: But be ye
> Transformed by the renewing of your mind, that ye

> May prove what is that good, And acceptable,
> And perfect, will of God
> Romans 12:2

By the power of the cross, the flesh with its works and sinful nature has also been made crucified and dead unto us. We have also been crucified and made dead unto the flesh with its works and sinful nature. These things have no more power and dominion over our lives any more in Christ. And in no way are these things made to have dominion over our lives in Christ (Romans 6:3-14).

We therefore, have to learn and position ourselves by faith in Christ to live in a way that would not give room for the flesh, the world and sin to dominate us again. The word of God says and reveals through what the apostle Paul taught us;

> This I say, walk in the Spirit
> And ye shall not fulfill the lust of the flesh
> For the flesh lusteth against the Spirit
> And the Spirit against the flesh and these are contrary
> The one to the other so that ye cannot
> Do the things that ye would
> Galatians 5:16-17

Being spiritually crucified with Christ by his cross, we have been made dead with all our past also crucified with Christ. It is a faithful saying to know and believe that Christ Jesus in going to the cross took all our past with him. We need not hold on to them, though the enemy would seek sometimes to use our past to challenge our faith and salvation; let him know that you are no more the old person whom he used to fool about. And even more; we have also been made resurrected and raised up with Christ by God. The bible speaks to encourage us in this way;

> Know ye not, that so many of us
> As were baptized into Jesus Christ were baptized
> Into his death? Therefore we are buried with him

By baptism into death: that like as Christ was raised up
From the dead by the glory of the Father, even so
We also should walk in newness of life.
Romans 6:1-4

For if we have been planted together
In the likeness of his death, we shall be also in
The likeness of his resurrection: Knowing this, that
Our old man is crucified with him, that the body of sin
Might be destroyed, that henceforth we should not serve sin
Romans 6:5-6
(Romans 6:14)

... And hath raised us up together,
And made us sit together in heavenly
Places in Christ Jesus:
Ephesians 2:6

We are a new creation in Christ. Knowing that we have died and risen up with our Lord is a key to understanding the new creation or the born again personality and its lifestyle with the resurrection power of Christ in him (Ephesians 1:18). It is here that the old things are passed away, dead and gone forever having been nailed to the cross by Christ. What is left ahead after being born again as a new creation is the newness of life in the glory unto which we are resurrected to live in Christ and unto God.

Likewise reckon ye also yourselves
To be dead indeed unto sin, but alive unto God
Through Jesus Christ our Lord
Romans 6:11

For as much then as Christ hath suffered
For us in the flesh, arm yourselves likewise with
The same mind: for he that hath suffered in the flesh
Hath ceased from sin; that he no longer should live

> The rest of his time in the flesh to the lusts of men,
> But to the will of God
> 1Peter 4:1-2

It is no more us, neither is it our own lives anymore but the life of Christ into which we have been baptized that needs to manifest in and through us. He has indeed become the life flow in us. It is him that needs to be demonstrated by the power of the Holy Spirit which has been given for us to become the children of God (John 1:12). It is just as the apostle Paul put it concerning himself;

> I am crucified with Christ
> Nevertheless I live; yet not I but Christ liveth in me
> And the life which I now live in the flesh I live by
> The faith of the Son of God who loved me
> And gave himself for me
> Galatians 2:20
> (Romans 6:4-8; Colossians 3:1-4)

Though the apostle Paul might be referring to himself, it is a revelation scripture which is also applicable to everyone who is born again and is in Christ as a new creation. It is in the light of all these that the cross of Christ has come to symbolize and represent many things in many ways of life. But unto the believer in Christ especially, it is the power of God to save mankind.

Though there may be many other things of which the cross of Christ might represent and symbolized, we would not be able to put all and everything into this little book. However, some of them do include the following;

SELF-DENIAL

The cross of Christ is a symbol but it is also a place of self-denial for the purposes of God in terms of the gospel. This is due to the many various denials that Christ himself had to face and go through by his own nation and the world which he came to die for. Many a time references of Christ being denied and betrayed are centered on the only common one by the apostle Peter after Jesus Christ was arrested (Luke 22:54-62). But least do we fail to realize somehow; and I believe it is good to know also, that Jesus Christ our Lord and Saviour lived in constant denial throughout his life on earth even by his own people. The bible says that he came unto his own but his own received him not (John 1:11). Judas's betrayal was in itself a form of denying the Lord (Luke 22:1-6, 47-48).

Denial was not a strange thing to the Lord. He himself predicted of that which was going to happen to him in terms of betrayal and denial from both Judas and Peter; for the bible says that our Lord is someone who knew and still do know the heart of men and what is inside of their heart as the bible reveals;

> But Jesus did not commit himself unto them,
> Because he knew all men, and needed not that any
> Should testify of man: for he knew what was in man
> John 2:24-25

Then again the Lord spoke concerning some of them that listened to him without believing what he said;

> It is the spirit that quickeneth;
> The flesh profiteth nothing: the words that I speak
> Unto you, they are spirit, and they are life.
> But there are some of you that believe not.
> For Jesus knew from the beginning who they were
> That believed not, and who should betray him.
> John 6:63-64

Even while the Lord hanged on the cross, he was being denied by them that stood afar to watch the crucifixion among whom were his own people (Luke 23:35-37).

However, the cross's symbolism or place of self-denial is unto sin, the flesh and the world with its lust. It is always for the sake of Christ and his word that we should deny ourselves. It is also a self-denial for the sake of the kingdom of God. We deny ourselves in order to pursue the things for which the Lord Jesus Christ through the cross purchased and made available unto us. In his teaching concerning the cross as a place of this self-denial, the Lord taught us this way as his disciples;

> And when he had called the people unto him
> With his disciples also he said unto them, whosoever will
> Come after me Let him deny himself and take up his cross
> And follow me for whosoever will save his life shall lose it
> But whosoever shall lose his life for my sake
> And the gospel's, the same shall save it
> Mark 8:34-35
> (Luke 9:23)

It is one way or the other; one cannot take up the cross to follow Christ unless he or she denies him or herself; and if you are a true follower of the master purposed to carry the cross, you cannot help but to deny yourself. The simplicity is that, the flesh cannot carry the cross and when the cross could be carried; it meant that the flesh was already dead. One truth is that, our Lord Jesus Christ was already dead to the world, sin and the flesh even before he went to the cross. Otherwise he couldn't have carried the cross. My brother or sister in Christ, or whoever is reading this book; it does not take sin, the flesh or the world to carry the cross. Deny yourself of these things in Jesus' name.

We as his followers therefore have to learn and accept self-denial as part of our lives in Christ so that we would be well prepared and positioned should we be denied by others for the sake of Christ. We deny ourselves of the flesh and its works or lusts by the power of the Holy Spirit of God that dwells in us, as we carry our cross to follow him. It is good to know that the Holy Spirit has not been given unto us just only to speak in tongues; but by him also, God the Father raises up a standard against the flesh which can be considered as an enemy of the cross. The bible says in the book of Isaiah;

> So shall thy fear the name of the Lord
> From the west and his glory from the rising of the sun
> When the enemy shall come in like a flood
> The Spirit of the Lord shall lift up
> A standard against him
> Isaiah 59:19

Let us never forget that the flesh is also an enemy to our spiritual life. The bible which is the word of God reveals that we are spiritual beings and therefore need to live and walk in the spirit (Galatians 5:25) in order to be led by the Spirit (Romans 8:14; Galatians 5:18) in every area of our lives as the word of God encourages us by the following scripture;

> This I say then
> Walk in the Spirit and ye shall
> Not fulfill the lust of the flesh
> Galatians 5:16

Again by the Holy Spirit also, we as the followers of Christ do mortify the deeds of the flesh (Romans 8:11-13; Galatians 5:24; Romans 6:3-6; Colossians 3:1-4). This is because the flesh and the lusts thereof are in constant struggle with our spirit (Galatians 5:17), but the bible says that we are not in flesh to be indebted or influenced by the flesh with its deeds and lusts. In this case we are not to make any room for the flesh.

Then on one occasion, a young man came to Jesus Christ to seek for the way of salvation, and when he had asked Jesus how he could obtain it; this is what the bible says as in response from the Lord;

> Then Jesus beholding him loved him;
> And said unto him one thing thou lackest; go thy way,
> Sell whatsoever thou hast and give to the poor
> And thou shalt have treasure in heaven and
> Come take up your cross and follow me
> Mark 10:21 (Matthew 16:24; John 12:26; John 10:27)

And with the taking up of our own cross; it simply means that we continue to crucify the things which are already made crucified by Christ on the cross for us, so that we don't have to live by them and with them anymore. Self-denial or denying oneself and of course its lusts, involves letting go off the many things that has to do with the old sinful, dead and fallen nature of man in relations with life in the worldly sense. In other words, self-denial or denying oneself is for the purpose and the things that enable the salvation of our souls or the soul of man to find the needed rest in God. It is to let go off that kind of "Me or My, Myself and I" sort of personality for the newness of personality which we have received in Christ as new Creations. The personality of the "Me or My, Myself and I" is what could be referred to as the body of sin. It is the nature and center of all pride and iniquities. This is that which the bible says is crucified with Christ on the cross (Romans 6:6). So the bible says;

> For what shall it profit a man
> If he shall gain the whole world and loose his own soul
> Or what shall a man give in exchange for his soul?
> Mark 8:36-37

However, the greatest self-denial that can be characterized with the cross of Christ as a symbol and a place of self-denial is that of the Lord himself. Many do not realize but our Lord had to deny himself before he could carry his cross to the place called Golgotha for him to be crucified there. Remember, no flesh or self can carry the cross; because if we understand it very well, carrying the cross is a form of glorifying God in the body or the flesh by the suffering it goes through for the sake of God's will, plan and purpose. And the word of God reveals that no flesh can glory in the Lord's presence (1Corinthians 1:29). The flesh has to die.

First of all, our body is or supposed to be the temple of the living God;

> What? Know ye not that your body is
> The temple of the Holy Ghost which is in you,

> Which ye have of God, and ye are not your own?
> For ye are bought with a price: therefore
> Glorify God in your body, and in
> Your spirit, which are God's
> 1Corinthians 6:19-20

In reference to the Lord's betrayal by Judas Iscariot, and his subsequent death on the cross, the Lord made it clear unto us how that his death was unto the glory of the Father. So that by his death, the Father will be glorified for him also to be glorified in the Father (John 13:23-32) and by our death with him we would also be brought into the glory of God (Hebrews 2:10).

I personally believe that our Lord in his prayer at the garden of Gethsemane was dealing a last blow to the self or the flesh which could have stood in his way to fulfill the Father's will, plan and purpose of salvation for mankind (Matthew 26:36-46). Again our Lord had to deny himself of all his glory to come down from heaven for the plans and purposes of God to be fulfilled on earth by dying shamefully on the cross. The apostle Paul narrates in his letter to the Philippians church;

> Let this mind be in you which was in Christ Jesus
> Who being in the form of God thought it not robbery
> To be equal with God; but made himself of no reputation
> And took upon him the form of a servant, and was made
> In the likeness of men, and being found in fashion as a man
> He humbled himself and became obedient unto death
> Even the death of the cross
> Philippians 2:5-8

And death on the cross was considered as a curse (Galatians 3:13). Oh Yes, our Lord denied himself of his entire glorious heavenly attributes to come down from heaven to the earth to do the Father's will (Hebrews 10:4-7; John 6:38; John 4:34).

We all are also purposed by God in Christ to do his will, pursue his plans and purpose on the earth and in this world. As we do the will of God and pursue his plan and purpose in Christ on earth and in this world, we are actually in the state of denying the self and its lusts.

The purpose of self-denial is also for Christ to be formed in us. The apostle Paul in his letter to the Galatians church revealed it concerning having Christ to be formed in us. He said to the Galatians;

> My little children,
> Of whom I travail again until
> Christ be formed in you
> Galatians 4:19

So just having Christ in us is not enough. Christ has to come alive and be formed in us. That is when we can get conformed into his image as sons of God as the bible reveals;

> For whom he did foreknow,
> He also did predestinate to be conformed
> To the image of his Son, that he might be
> The firstborn among many brethren
> Romans 8:29

Self-denial or denying ourselves is purposed for Christ to be increased in us just as in the case of John the Baptist who declared concerning the Lord Jesus Christ;

> He must increase, but I must decrease
> John 3:30

The more we get decreased through death to the flesh, sin and the world with their lustful deeds; we at the same time make room or place for Christ to increase in and through us.

Self-denial is purposed for Christ to be manifested in and through us. Unless Christ is able to manifest in and through us, we might as well not be able to live and fulfill God's purposes for our lives in Christ. Do not forget the truth that it is Christ who becomes our lives (Colossians 3:3-4) to live and manifest in and through us when we become born again (Galatians 2:20; Philippians 1:20). The bible states;

> For the earnest expectation of
> The Creature waiteth for the manifestation
> Of the Sons of God
> Romans 8:19

And the manifestation of the true Sons of God is that which will also bring about the fulfillment of God's purpose and glory in our lives, which also would enable us to overcome and destroy the works of the devil which is sin. The bible brings it across in this way as the apostle John reveals;

> He that committeth sin is of the devil;
> For the devil sinneth from the beginning.
> For this purpose the Son of God Was manifested,
> That he might destroy the works of the devil.
> 1 John 3:8

Self-denial or denying the Self is purposed for Christ to be revealed in and through us. As we die to the flesh and its lusts for Christ to manifest; he is also revealed in and through us by our thoughts, deeds, actions and utterances.

This is just like the case of the apostle Paul after his personal encounter with the Lord Jesus Christ on his way to persecute the Christians in Damascus. He declares of how God revealed Christ in him and which totally affected his whole personality and life to even begin preaching Christ. He stated;

> But when it pleased God,
> Who separated me from my mother's womb
> And called me by his grace, to reveal his Son in me,
> That I might preach him among the heathen;
> Immediately I conferred not with flesh and blood:
> Galatians 1:15-16

When we are decreased and Christ has been increased and being manifested in and through our lives through self-denial; it is like he becomes our lives so that as he is also being revealed in and through us, we share in the fullness of his glory that is being manifested. The bible says;

> For ye are dead,
> And your life is hid with Christ in God.
> When Christ, who is our life, shall appear,
> Then shall ye also appear with him in glory.
> Colossians 3:3-4

> And if children, then heirs; heirs of God
> and joint- heirs with Christ; if so be that we suffer with him,
> That we may be also glorified together
> Romans 8:17

The word "appear" in the scripture above is not in terms of the second coming. It is in reference to when the Christ in you would be revealed for him to be seen in his glory through you right here on earth (Colossians 1:27; 2 Corinthians 3:17-18)

> This becomes like having put on Christ as the bible reveals it;
> But put ye on the Lord Jesus Christ,
> And make not provision for the flesh,
> To fulfill the lusts thereof
> Romans 13:14

> For as many of you
> As have been baptized into Christ
> Have put on Christ
> Galatians 3:27

In other words, it is for us to be clothed with Christ so that when we show up anywhere at any time, people would see the reflection of the Christ in our lives instead of us. But one may ask how would

Christ be seen in and through us by others? In and through the way we would think, speak, act and react to situations and circumstances as well as to people in life; Christ can be seen.

This would be like in the case of the apostles when they were arrested and brought before the Jewish leaders for preaching in the name of Jesus Christ. The bible says;

> Now when they saw the boldness of Peter and John,
> And perceived that they were unlearned and
> Ignorant men, they marveled;
> And they took knowledge of them,
> That they had been with Jesus
> Acts 4:13
> (Acts 10:38)

Denying ourselves to decrease for Christ to increase in us is a way of how Christ becomes profitable unto us (Galatians 5:2). It is also a way for Christ to be glorified in us and for us to be glorified in him and with him as the apostle Paul's letter to the Church in Thessalonica reveals;

> That the name of our Lord Jesus Christ
> May be glorified in you, and ye in him,
> According to the grace of our God
> And the Lord Jesus Christ
> 2 Thessalonians 1:12
> (John 17:1-5; 1 Peter 4:14; Mark 8:38)

By denying ourselves in order to be decreased for Christ to increase; we learn to die every day to the flesh; and by dying every day to the flesh, Christ gets increased for his life to come forth and be manifested in and through us so we can end up living a Christ like life. In this way, we end up getting conformed into his image and his likeness. This is how the apostle Paul spoke about the daily dying of the believer for Christ to increase in him;

Who shall separate us from the love of Christ?
Shall tribulation, or distress, or persecution, or famine,
Or nakedness, or danger, or sword? As it is written,
"For your sake we are being killed all the daylong;
We are regarded as sheep to be slaughtered."
Romans 8:35-36

For we which live are always delivered
Unto death for Jesus'sake, that the life also
Of Jesus might be made manifest in our mortal flesh.
2 Corinthians 4:11
(Galatians 2:20; Philippians 1:20; 1Corinthians 6:20)

PERSECUTION, AFFLICTION AND SUFFERING

The cross of Christ is a symbol but it is also a place of persecution, afflictions and suffering for the sake of Christ and the will of God. It is one of the important things to know that Jesus Christ came on earth to do the Father's will. For that matter, it was the doing of the Father's will that took our Lord and Saviour to the cross to suffer the ordeal of crucifixion. The following scriptures are just some of the few references that reveal this;

Wherefore when he cometh into the world,
He saith, Sacrifice and offering thou wouldest not,
But a body hast thou prepared me:
In burnt offerings and sacrifices for sin
Thou hast had no pleasure.
Then said I, Lo, I come
(In the volume of the book it is written of me,)
To do thy will, O God
Hebrews 10:5-7

... He went away again the second time,
And prayed, saying, O my Father, if this cup

> May not pass away from me, except I drink it,
> Thy will be done.
> Matthew 26:42

When we call into memory the persecution and the sufferings in and through which our Lord Jesus Christ went; we can also somehow understand what the Father's will concerning the cross was. Not only that, it also reflects the persecution, the affliction and sufferings the early Church encountered and went through for their faith in Jesus Christ. The Lord said to the early disciples;

> Verily, verily, I say unto you,
> The servant is not greater than his lord;
> Neither he that is sent greater than he that sent him.
> John 13:16

> Remember the word that I said unto you,
> The servant is not greater than his lord.
> If they have persecuted me, they will also persecute you;
> If they have kept my saying, they will keep yours also.
> John 15:20

> If the world hate you,
> Ye know that it hated me before it hated you.
> If ye were of the world, the world would love his own
> But because ye are not of the world, but I have chosen
> You out of the world, therefore the world hateth you.
> John 15:18-19

The apostle Paul in his letter to his son in the faith, Timothy said;

> Yea and all that will live godly
> In Christ Jesus shall suffer persecution
> 2 Timothy 3:12

Saul, who later became the apostle Paul, is one person who persecuted the Church of Jesus Christ. In his words of testimony to the Corinthian church after he became born again and a follower and servant of the Lord Jesus Christ he said;

> For I am the least of the apostles
> That I am not meet to be called an apostle
> Because I persecuted the church of God
> 1 Corinthians 15:9

It was on one of his persecuting missions that he Saul had a direct encounter with Jesus Christ. This divine encounter brought the apostle Paul to a turnabout through which he became a follower of Christ. The bible narrates the apostle's encounter with the Lord as this;

> And as he journeyed, he came near Damascus
> And suddenly there shined round about him a light
> From heaven and he fell to the earth and heard a voice
> Saying unto him Saul, Saul why persecutest thou me?
> And he said who art thou, Lord? And the Lord said
> I am Jesus whom thou persecutest: It is hard for thee
> To kick against the pricks and he trembling and
> Astonished said Lord, what wilt thou have me to do?
> And the Lord said unto him, Arise and go
> Into the city, and it shall be told thee
> What thou must do
> Acts 9:3-6

However, when after Saul now Paul, had come to know Jesus Christ as his Lord and Saviour; he himself also encountered and went through persecutions because of his faith. But with the persecutions that he went through in serving the Lord; he could also joyfully encourage the Church or the Body of Christ as far as persecution is concerned in serving the Lord. He said to the church in Rome;

> Bless them that persecute you
> Bless and curse not
> Romans 12:14

And again in sharing some of his experience in persecution, he said to the Corinthian church;

> We are troubled on every side yet not distressed
> We are perplexed, but not in despaired, persecuted
> But not forsaken, cast down but not destroyed
> Always bearing about in the body the dying of the Lord Jesus
> That the life also of Jesus might be made manifest in our body
> For we which live are always delivered unto death
> For Jesus sake that the life also of Jesus might
> Be made manifest in our mortal flesh
> 2 Corinthians 4:8-11
> (Galatians 2:20; 1 Corinthians 15:51-55)

You see, persecution, afflictions and tribulations for the sake of Jesus Christ are a divine way of manifesting the life of Christ in us. Persecution, afflictions and tribulations for the sake of Jesus Christ seem to be a normal part of our Christian lives and reward us in our heavenly account. These are some of the things that cause us to decrease and die to the flesh that Christ would increase, come alive and manifest in and through our lives like the apostle Paul who declared;

> I am crucified with Christ:
> Nevertheless I live; yet not I, but Christ liveth in me:
> And the life which I now live in the flesh I live
> By the faith of the Son of God, who loved me
> And gave himself for me
> Galatians 2:20

I believe it is more the reason why the apostle Paul could rejoice, and encourage the church to also rejoice in persecutions if it is only for the sake of Christ. And also, if the persecutions we encounter and go through are for the sake of truth; and to live unto God by faith in Jesus Christ. The apostle Paul himself experienced persecutions for the sake of Christ. These persecutions seem to have become a normality of his life in Christ, and we can at least make reference with him and Silas in the prison which also came about for the sake of the gospel (Acts 16:1-40). He said to the Roman church about how facing and going through tribulation is possible but only in and through Christ;

> By whom also we have access by faith
> Into this grace wherein we stand and rejoice in hope
> Of the glory of God and not only so, but we glory in tribulations
> Also knowing that tribulation worketh patience
> Romans 5:2-3
> (James 1:2-4; Hebrews 10:36; Hebrews 6:11-12; Luke 21:19)

However, encountering and going through persecution, afflictions and suffering for the sake of Christ and our faith in him does not go without rewards. Our Lord Jesus Christ helped to throw some light on the rewards that account on our behalf in the heavenly places or in heaven so that we never have to give up of our faith, trust and confidence as Christians when we go through persecution, affliction or tribulation for his sake and that of righteousness. He encouraged us with these words;

> Blessed are they which are persecuted
> For righteousness sake, for theirs is the kingdom of God
> Blessed are ye, when men shall revile you and persecute
> You and shall say all manner of evil against you falsely
> For my sake, rejoice and be exceedingly glad
> For great is your reward in heaven
> For so persecuted they the prophets
> Which were before you
> Matthew 5:10-12
> (1 Peter 4:12-14; Matthew 13:20-21)

And then again, the Lord answered to reply and encourage us concerning persecution while he was with the early disciples. This was in answer to Simon Peter's question which also throws light on how being persecuted for the sake of Christ can be a normal part of the Christian faith but also with rewards.

> Then Peter began to say unto him
> Lo, we have left all and have followed thee
> And Jesus answered and said verily I say unto you,
> There is no man that hath left house, or brethren or sisters
> Or father or mother or wife, or children or lands for my sake
> And the gospel's But he shall receive an hundredfold now
> In this time, houses and brethren and sisters and mothers,
> And children and lands with persecutions;
> And in the world to come
> Eternal life
> Mark 10:28-30

Our Lord Jesus Christ even went on to encourage us as his church and body to pray for them that are persecuting and would persecute us for his sake. He also made it clear unto us, how that being persecuted and afflicted for his sake, establishes our divine nature and position as the children of our Father who is in heaven. He taught us this way;

> Ye have heard that it hath been said
> Thou shalt love thy neighbour and hate thine enemy
> But I say unto you, love your enemies bless them that
> Curse you, do good to them that hate you and pray for
> Them which despitefully use you and persecute you
> That ye may be the children of your father
> Who is in heaven: for he maketh his sun to rise
> On the evil and on the good, and sendeth
> Rain on the just and on the unjust
> Matthew 5:43-45

It is good to know that all that will live a godly life in Christ and suffer for his sake shall encounter some sort of persecution, afflictions and tribulations as the apostle Paul reveals it unto us;

> For unto you it is given in the behalf of Christ,
> Not only to believe on him, but also to suffer for
> His sake; having the same conflict which
> Ye saw in me, and now hear to be in me.
> Philippians 1:29

But the good news is that the Lord is always there to see us through them all as he has promised never to leave us nor forsake us (2 Timothy 3:11-12; Psalm 34:19; Hebrews 13:5-6). By the promise of his ever presence with us, the Lord causes us to triumph (2Corinthians 2:14). He also causes us to be winners, over comers and more than conquerors (Romans 8:33-39); which comes by the power of his might (Ephesians 6:10) and the help of the Holy Ghost (Zachariah 4:6; Acts 1:8).

Persecution, affliction and tribulation as well as suffering for the sake of Christ and for our faith in him; and also for his word and his righteousness are all sorts of means by which we share in the sufferings of Christ. And the bible says that, all these persecutions go to work patience in us;

> And not only so, but we glory in tribulation also
> Knowing that tribulation worketh patience
> Romans 5:3
> (James 1:2-4; Luke 21:19).

Again, persecution, affliction and tribulation for the sake of Christ, as well as for the sake of our faith in him, his word and his righteousness also contributes to revealing the glory of God that is upon us in Christ. The apostle Peter who also witnessed or experienced the sufferings of Christ (1 Peter 5:1) encourages us with this scripture;

Beloved, think it not strange concerning
The fiery trial which is to try you as though some strange
Thing happened to you, but rejoice inasmuch as ye are partakers
Of Christ's sufferings that when his glory shall be revealed
Ye may be glad also with exceeding joy
1 Peter 4:12-13
(Isaiah 60:1-2; Hebrews 2:6-7; Colossians 3:3-4; Philippians 1:29)

Persecution, affliction and tribulation for the sake of Christ, for the sake of our faith in him, as well as for his word and his righteousness all contributes to revealing the Spirit of God and his glory that is upon us in Christ. Again the apostle Peter shares this insight with us through the following scripture;

If ye be reproached for the name of Christ
Happy are ye, for the spirit of glory and of God
Resteth upon you, on their part he is evil spoken of
But on your part he is glorified
1 Peter 4:14
(Isaiah 61:1-3; Luke 4:18-19; Isaiah 10:27)

MOCKERY

The cross of Christ is the symbol or a place of mockery. Right from the beginning even before Jesus Christ was arrested until he painfully walked his way towards the cross for his crucifixion; he was whipped, kicked and spat upon. He was torn apart and degraded to a mockery. However, the mockery of our Lord Jesus Christ was not new to him. Knowing why he came and where he was heading to, he had earlier on prophesied this state of mockery to his disciples as the bible records;

Then he took unto him the twelve
And said unto them behold, we go up to Jerusalem
And all things that are written by the prophets concerning
The Son of man shall be accomplished, for he shall be delivered

Unto the gentiles and shall be mocked and spitefully entreated
And spitted on and they shall scourge him and put him to death
And on the third day he shall rise again
Luke 18:31-33

The bible gives instances of the Lord's mockery which have come to imply or simplify the cross as a symbol of mockery. One example is when Jesus Christ was arrested and sent to the governor's house where he was left at the mercy of the soldiers. There the bible records how the Lord Jesus Christ suffered maltreatments in their hands with all kinds of abuses just to mock him. This is what the bible says concerning it;

Then the soldiers of the governor took
Jesus into the common hall and gathered unto him the whole
Band of soldiers and they stripped him and put on him a
scarlet robe,
And when they had platted a crown of thorns and a reed in his
Right hand and they bowed the knee before him and mocked
Him saying, Hail King of the Jews! And they spit upon him,
And took the reed and smote him on the head, and after
They have mocked him they took the robe off from him
And put his own raiment on him and led him
Away to crucify him
Matthew 27:27-31

He was mocked by the chief priests, the scribes and the elders of the Jews as the bible says;

Likewise the chief priests mocking him
With the scribes and elders said he saved others,
Himself he cannot save, if he be the king of Israel, let him
Now come down from the cross and we will believe him
He trusted in God, let him deliver him now
If he will have him, for he said,
I am the Son of God Matthew 27:41-43

Our Lord was mocked in every area of his life and it is very important to know that we as his followers would be made a mockery at sometimes in our lives as well concerning our faith in him. We will be mocked for the sake of his name. We will be mocked for the sake of his word and even for the sake of his calling and ministry upon our lives. This is not to be negative but to faithfully agree with the Lord as he has taught us it would come. This is how our Lord taught us through the disciples where he said;

> The disciple is not above his master
> Nor the servant above his Lord, it is enough for
> The disciple that he be as his master and the servant as his lord
> If they have called the master of the house Beelzebub
> How much more shall they call them
> Of his household
> Matthew 10:24-25
> (Luke 6:40; John 13:16)

Then on another occasion the Lord said to the weeping women as he carried his cross towards Golgotha where he would be crucified;

> For if they do these things in a green tree
> What shall be done in the dry?
> Luke 23:31

In other words, if such things have been meted unto him, the same thing will be meted unto his followers. This is something we can see through the lives of the believers in the early Church and even through to these days in certain countries around the world where believers in Christ are persecuted. If we as his followers will remind ourselves and consider some of the Lord's words of warning, we would always be prepared to face circumstances in the power of his might; just as he also encountered, faced and overcame them triumphantly. The apostle Paul in the course of his missions also experienced this mockery as we can read the story in the book of Acts chapter 17. This is when he had taken the opportunity to share

Christ and his resurrection power to a group of Athenians as he stood in the midst of Mars' hill. Though some believed, the bible records that when they had heard of the resurrection of the dead, some mocked (Acts 17:32).

The good news is that, once our Lord Jesus Christ was able to face and overcome mockery, we also can overcome mockery by the power of his might and the Holy Spirit. He assured us;

>These things I have spoken unto you,
>That in me ye might have peace, in the world
>Ye shall have tribulation: but be of good cheer;
>I have overcome the world.
>John 16:33

In following his steps to suffer through mockery for the sake of Christ, the apostle Peter puts it this way perhaps, as a means of getting our minds prepared;

>Forasmuch then as Christ hath suffered
>For us in the flesh, arm yourselves likewise
>With the same mind: for he that hath suffered
>In the flesh hath ceased from sin;
>1Peter4:1
>(1Peter 1:13)

In a similar way, the apostle Paul in speaking to the Philippians' church puts it this way;

>Let this mind be in you,
>Which was also in Christ Jesus: Who, being
>In the form of God, thought it not robbery
>To be equal with God: But made himself
>Of no reputation, and took upon him
>The form of a servant, and was
>Made in the likeness of men:
>Philippians 2:5-7

CRUCIFIXION TO THE OLD, DEAD AND FALLEN NATURE

The cross of Christ is a symbol but also a place of crucifixion and death to the old and fallen sinful nature of man. Though not a sinner, Christ died the death of a sinner by taking upon himself the sins of the whole human race unto the cross. And by doing that, it was as if the sinner himself actually accompanied Christ to be crucified also on the cross with him. This makes the believer in Christ to be made spiritually dead unto sin and its lusts. Dead unto sin; he no longer responds to sin and its lust. Neither does sin and its lusts have any effect on him that is in Christ. The bible speaks to explain it in this way;

> What shall we say then?
> Shall we continue in sin, that grace may abound?
> God forbid. How shall we, that are dead to sin,
> Live any longer therein? Know ye not, that so
> Many of us as were baptized into Jesus Christ
> Were baptized into his death?
> Romans 6:1-4

It is death to the world and its lusts (1John 2:15-17; John 8:23; John 15:18-21; John 17:15-18). It is death to the flesh with all its cares and lusts (Galatians 5:24; 1Peter 4:1-2).

In other words it represents the crucifixion and the death to all the old, dead and fallen past of a person's life; no matter how sinful or evil it might seem or have been, which passes away when a person becomes a new creation in Christ (2 Corinthians 5:17). This divine mystery was established the moment Christ finished his works on the cross and said it is finished. The bible says;

> When Jesus therefore had received
> The vinegar, he said, IT IS FINISHED
> And he bowed his head and gave up the ghost
> John 19:30

It was finished with sin and its curses of sickness and diseases reigning in the life of man. It was finished with the curses of poverty, lack and leanness in the life of mankind. Yes, it was finished with the fear of death and its rule of terror over man's life. Oh yes, it was finished with the devil taking mankind captive at his own will. And yes, it was finished with the holding on to the past, which the enemy takes advantage of to build strongholds in the minds of so many people and hold them in bondage.

Now, it is good to know and believe that, 'IT IS FINISHED' as Jesus said it, is not only meant for the past. It was said with an eternal tone which means that whatever power, plan and purpose which the devil had, have and shall forever have to want man to fall out in covenant relations with God has forever and ever been dealt with and come to an end because of the works of Christ on the cross and his shed precious blood to redeem us;

> Forasmuch as ye know that
> Ye were not redeemed with corruptible things,
> As silver and gold, from your vain conversation
> Received by tradition from your fathers;
> But with the precious blood of Christ,
> As of a lamb without blemish and without spot:
> 1 Peter 1:18-19

It was through Christ's work on the cross of Calvary that his precious blood was shed for the sins of the whole world. The blood causes every flow of Satan's activities to cease and be overcome.

As Jesus Christ went to the cross and hanged on it in the human form or body (Philippians 2:5-8), that human form or body contained or bore every works of the flesh and the sinful nature of all mankind with its curses, that God the Father intended to have nailed on the cross once and for all. It is also good to know and believe that, in the realm of the Spirit, the flesh with its entire works and lusts and the world with all its cares are crucified with Christ on the cross where they have been overcome. And the apostle Paul makes us to understand it this way;

> Know ye not that so many of us as were baptized
> Into Jesus Christ were baptized into his death (of the cross)
> Therefore we are buried with him by baptism
> Into death: that like as Christ was raised up from
> The dead by the glory of the Father
> Even so we also should walk in newness of life
> Romans 6:3-4

So therefore now in Christ, it would be more of a blessing for every believer to learn by faith and live without looking back to their past lives of shame, guilt and condemnation; but to learn and take hold of the power and authority made available unto them in and through the works of Christ on the cross by which every believer in Christ Jesus can reign and rule in life over the devil, sin, the flesh and the world. Once again the apostle Paul, who understood, received and walked in this revelation, encourages us with his life after he became the Lord's servant. He said;

> Brethren, I count not myself to have
> Apprehended: but this one thing I do
> Forgetting those things which are behind
> And reaching forth unto those things which are before
> I press toward the mark for the prize of the
> High calling of in Christ Jesus
> Philippians 3:13-14

Like the apostle Paul who knew no turning back, we should also keep looking forward to press on unto the higher calling that is in Christ for us. This is only possible as we let go off the past and look up unto our Lord who is the Author and finisher of our faith (Hebrews 12:1-3). For the bible says that the Just shall live by faith, and living by faith means no turning back but continuously looking unto Christ. The bible says;

> Now the just shall live by faith, but if any man draw back
> My soul shall have no pleasure in him

But we are not of them who draw back unto perdition
But of them that believe to the saving of the soul
Hebrews 10:38-39
(Hebrews 12:2-3)

And our Lord Jesus Christ taught us in one of his conversations with the early disciples this way;

And Jesus said unto him
No man, having put his hand to the plough
And looking back, is fit for the kingdom of God
Luke 9:62

SUFFERING AND PAIN IN THE FLESH

The cross of Christ is a symbol and a place of suffering and pain in the flesh and to the flesh. In talking about the Lord Jesus Christ as he walked towards the place of crucifixion, the bible narrates;

And he bearing his cross went forth
Into a place called the place of a skull,
Which is called in the Hebrew, Golgotha
Where they crucified him and two other with him
On either side one and Jesus in the midst
John 19:17-18

Every suffering and every pain that our Lord Jesus Christ bore in his life on earth here right to the cross, he bore them in the flesh. And every suffering and pain he bore in the flesh was for us. And yet again, every pain and suffering our Lord Jesus Christ bore was an example for us to follow. After bowing and humbling himself to wash the feet of the disciples, our Lord says that was an example he gave to us; as example which he encouraged us to do. This is how the bible tells us;

> So after he had washed their feet
> And had taken his garments and was set again
> He said unto them, know ye what I have done
> Unto you, ye call me Master and Lord, and ye say well
> For so I am, if I then your Lord and Master have washed
> Your feet, ye also ought to wash one another's feet
> For I have given you example that you should
> Do as I have done to you
> John 13:12-15

Then the apostle Peter also encouraged the Church concerning the suffering and pain they would encounter and go through in the flesh, and see it as an example unto us from the Lord. The apostle Peter put it this way;

> For even hereunto were ye called because
> Christ also suffered for us, leaving us an example
> That ye should follow his steps
> 1 Peter 1:21

Then again, every suffering and pain that our Lord Jesus Christ bore in the flesh, he bore them for us. This was in order to bring us to God as the bible says;

> For Christ also hath once suffered for sins
> The just for the unjust, that he might bring us
> To God, being put to death in the flesh
> But quickened by the Spirit
> 1 Peter 3:18

This means that, whenever we release our faith to stand in for righteousness, holiness and faithfulness in the word and unto the plans, purposes and will of God, the flesh will surely go through some sort of suffering and pain. But it is the more reason why we carry our cross to follow the Lord, so as to crucify every works of the flesh. However, the word of God faithfully warns us to gird the loins of our mind (1 Peter1:13) and arm ourselves in readiness to defeat and overcome the flesh and its lusts by pulling down strongholds of the flesh, sin and worldliness; to cast down imaginations and take captive of all and every thought that exalts itself against the knowledge of God (2 Corinthians 10:5). Once again the apostle Peter encourages us to arm ourselves with these words;

> Forasmuch then as Christ has suffered for us
> In the flesh, arm yourselves likewise with the same mind
> For he that hath suffered in the flesh
> Hath ceased from sin
> 1 Peter 4:1-2
> (Philippians 2:5-8)

It is the more reason why sin can have no more dominion over us in and through the flesh and its lusts (Romans 6:14; 1 John 3:9) because we are dead to the flesh and do not live according to the flesh in Christ (Romans 8:5, 12). It is like in the spirit and glory realm in Christ, our bodies no more respond to worldliness, sin and all the fleshly lusts (Romans 6:14)

However as Believers in Christ, we need to take up our divine responsibility to maintain our life and walk in the Spirit (Romans 8:9; Galatians 5:25) in order not to give place or make any room for the flesh (Galatians 5:16) by mortifying the deeds of the flesh through the Spirit (Romans 8:13) who quickens our mortal bodies against the flesh and its lusts of sin (Romans 8:11; John 6:63; 2 Corinthians 3:6) so that we can live a righteous and a holy life (1Peter 1:15-16), by presenting the members of our body as instruments of righteousness unto holiness (Romans 6:19) unto the glory of God (1 Corinthians 1:29)

> For the law of the Spirit of life in Christ
> Jesus hath made me free from
> The law of sin and death
> Romans 8:2
> (Romans 6:14)

HUMILIATION, REJECTION AND LONELINESS

The cross of Christ is a symbol and a place of humiliation, rejection and loneliness. The moment our Lord was arrested and was going through all the ordeals of mishandling in and through the hands of the various powers and authorities; it was the moment when he was humiliated, rejected and made to be alone and all on his own. His disciples had deserted him as he had predicted unto them earlier on;

> Then saith Jesus unto them
> All ye shall be offended because of me this night
> For it is written, I will smite the shepherd
> And the sheep of the flock shall be scattered abroad
> Matthew 26:30;

> Jesus answered them, do ye now believe?
> Behold, the hour cometh, yea
> Is now come that ye shall be scattered
> Every man to his own and shall leave me
> Alone, and yet I am not alone
> Because the Father is with me
> John 16; 31-32

Humiliated, rejected and made to be lonely in the hands of Pilate by the leaders of his own, the people proceeded to get him crucified as they chanted in unison for his crucifixion (Luke 23:21; John 19:6). And so humbled and humiliated in the hands of Pilate, the Lord was presented before the people after having been scourged (John 19:1-3);

> Then came Jesus forth wearing the crown
> Of thorns and the purple robe
> And Pilate said unto them, behold the man!
> When the chief priests therefore and officers
> Saw him they cried out saying, crucify him,

> Crucify him, Pilate said into them
> Take ye him and crucify him
> For I find no fault in him
> John 19; 5-6

Then again after an attempt to free Jesus Christ, Pilate came to enquire of the high priests who had not changed their mind to have Jesus Christ crucified. The bible says;

> And it was the preparation of the Passover
> And about the sixth hour and he said unto the Jews
> Behold your King! But they cried out
> Away with him, away with him, crucify him
> Pilate said unto them, shall crucify your King?
> The chief priests answered, we have no king but Caesar
> John 19:14-15

So therefore our Lord having gone through all the ordeals of suffering and pain; and having been rejected and given up unto crucifixion and all alone, carried his cross along the streets of Jerusalem to be crucified. But the greatest of all the rejection and loneliness came whiles the Lord hanged on the cross. It was the sixth hour and the bible records that darkness covered the whole land until the ninth hour. But this was also the moment when the sins of the whole world were placed upon him. At that particular moment the Father, who hates sin and could not look upon sin, had to let go off the hand of his only begotten and beloved Son whereby Jesus cried out unto the Father concerning having forsaken him. This is what the bible says;

> And at the ninth hour Jesus cried
> With a loud voice saying Eloi, Eloi, lamasabacthani
> Which is being interpreted, my God, my God
> Why hast thou forsaken me?
> Mark 15:34

DIVINE RECONCILIATION AND PEACE

The cross of Christ is a symbol and a place of divine reconciliation of peace with God and mankind. It is God's divine means of bringing mankind and all his creation back unto himself in and through Christ Jesus. This is how the bible reveals it;

> And all things are of God who has reconciled us
> To himself by Jesus Christ and has given to us
> The ministry of reconciliation
> 2 Corinthians 5:18

The cross is also a means and a place of God bringing peace unto man inand through Christ; so that people of every kindred, tongue and nation, Jew, Greek and Gentile; can come together to have peace with God and make peace with one another through fellowship. This is a union of divine fellowship which also embodies the Father, Son and the Holy Ghost (1 Corinthians 1:9; 2Corinthians 13:14; 1John 1:3).

The Holy Spirit by inspiration through the apostle Paul puts it this way concerning peace through the cross of Christ when he preached to the Ephesians Church;

> For he is our peace who hath made both one
> And hath broken down the middle wall of partition
> Between us; having abolished in his flesh the enmity
> Even the law of commandments contained in ordinances
> For to make in himself of twain one new man so making
> Peace and that he might reconcile both unto God
> In one body by the cross having slain the enmity
> Thereby
> Ephesians 2:14-16
> (Galatians 6:15; Galatians 5:5-6; Galatians 3:26-29; Colossians 3:10-11; Revelation 5:9-10)

And Our Lord is the Prince of peace…

> For unto us a child is born unto us a son is given
> And the government shall be upon his shoulder
> And his name shall be called Wonderful,
> Counselor, The mighty God,
> The everlasting Father, The Prince of Peace
> Isaiah 9:6-7

His kingdom is of peace…

> Of the increase of his government and peace
> There shall be no end, upon the throne of David
> And upon his kingdom, to order it and to
> Establish it with judgment and with justice
> From henceforth even forever. The zeal of
> The Lord of hosts will perform this
> Isaiah 9:7

> For the kingdom of God is not meat and drink
> But righteousness and peace and joy in the Holy Ghost
> For he that in these things serveth Christ
> Is acceptable to God, and approved of men
> Romans 14:17-18

At his birth, peace was announced and released to all men on earth…

> For unto you is born this day in the city of David
> A Saviour, which is Christ the Lord; and this shall be
> A sign unto you; Ye shall find the babe wrapped
> In swaddling clothes, lying in a manger.
> And suddenly there was with the angel
> A multitude of the heavenly host praising God,
> And saying, Glory to God in the highest,
> And on earth peace, good will toward men.
> Luke 2:11-14

He came to preach peace...

And that he might reconcile both unto God
In one body by the cross, having slain the enmity thereby:
And came and preached peace to you which were
Afar off, and to them that were nigh.
Ephesians 2:16-17

He came to give and make peace...

Peace I leave with you,
My peace I give unto you: not as the world giveth,
Give I unto you. Let not your heart be troubled, neither let it be afraid.
John 14:27

Having abolished in his flesh the enmity,
Even the law of commandments contained in ordinances;
For to make in himself of twain one new man, so making peace;
Ephesians 2:15

And they that sat at meat with him
Began to say within themselves, who is this
That forgiveth sins also? And he said to the woman,
Thy faith hath saved thee; go in peace.
Luke 7:49-50

And when the woman saw that she was not hid,
She came trembling, and falling down before him,
She declared unto him before all the people for what cause
She had touched him, and how she was healed immediately
And he said unto her, Daughter, Be of good comfort:
Thy faith hath made thee whole; go in peace.
Luke 8:47-48

He taught us to give and impart peace ...

And when ye come into an house, Salute it.
And if the house be worthy, let your peace come upon it:
But if it be not worthy, let your peace return to you.
Matthew 10:12-13
(Luke 10:5; Ephesians 6:13-15; Romans 10:15)

He taught us to be at peace and live peaceably with all men . . .

Recompense to no man evil for evil.
Provide things honest in the sight of all men.
If it be possible, as much as lieth in you, live peaceably
With all me
Romans 12:17-18

His peace as a weapon of warfare enables the Believer in Christ to walk and trample over serpents and scorpions and all the power of Satan...

And he said unto them,
I beheld Satan as lightning fall from heaven.
Behold, I give unto you power to tread on serpents
And scorpions, and over all the power of the enemy:
And nothing shall by any means hurt you.
Luke 10:18-19

And your feet shod with
The preparation of the gospel of peace;
Ephesians 6:15
And the God of peace
Shall bruise Satan under your feet shortly
The grace of our Lord Jesus Christ be with you. Amen.
Romans 16:20

The purpose of God making peace with man is for God to have himself a people of one body in and through Christ. It is a divine fellowship with one another with the purpose to build his church through love, unity and harmony (John 17:21-23). A body and a church against which no gates of Hades shall prevail (Matthew 16:18); but that his church would possess the divine power to conquer, win, overcome and possess the gates of the enemy (Luke 10:19; Genesis 22:16-17) with Satan bruised under the feet of God's people (Romans 16:20). A body of people that is redeemed and bought by the blood of Christ that was shed on the cross of Calvary (Colossians 1:20; 1Corinthians 6:20); and a people that is united, filled and anointed with the fire, power and anointing of the Holy Ghost or the Spirit of God (Ephesians 2:18-22).

Yes, by the cross God brought mankind into fellowship or communion with himself, with his Son and with his Holy Ghost (1Corinthians1:9; 1John 1:3; 2Corinthians 13:14).

Thus in Jesus Christ, we have peace with God (Romans 5:1). Hallelujah and glory be to God! A peace that reigns and rules the hearts and minds of them who are in Christ Jesus (Philippians 4:5-7)

And not only that, but even whiles on the cross, Christ himself brought some other people together as was in the case of his mother and another of his disciples called John who is also known as the Beloved Disciple. The bible records it this way;

> Now there stood by the cross of Jesus
> His mother and his mother's sister Mary the wife of Cleophas
> And Mary Magdalene When Jesus therefore saw his mother
> And the disciple Standing by whom he love, he said unto
> His mother Woman, behold thy son!
> Then said he to the disciple, behold thy mother
> And from that hour that disciple took
> Her unto His own home
> John 19:25-27

Another incident where people were made reconciled through the events of the cross of Christ was between Pilate and Herod who had been in enmity with one another before Christ's arrest, trial and crucifixion. The bible records it this way;

> And Herod with his men of war set him
> At nought, and mocked him, and arrayed him
> In a gorgeous robe, and sent him again to Pilate.
> And the same day Pilate and Herod were
> Made friends together: for before they
> Were at enmity between themselves
> (Luke 23:12)

These are but a few of what show and emphasize the divine reconciliatory power of the cross of Christ or as it is also known, the cross of Calvary.

Now it is good to know that once a person is in Christ, he or she becomes a child and heir of God with Christ as joint-heirs (Romans 8:17) and shares in everything with him. What the person in Christ shares with him includes his life before the cross (John 13:13-17; 1Peter 2:21-25; Philippians 2:5-8), his life on and at the cross (Romans 6:3-13), his life after and beyond the cross where he is glorified and made to sit at the right hand side of the Father in the heavenly places (Romans 8:9; Ephesians 2:6; 1Corinthians 6:17; Colossians 3:1-4).

GOD'S MANIFESTED LOVE

The cross of Christ is the symbol and a place of God's manifested love for mankind. The bible says;

> For God so loved the world that he gave
> His only begotten Son that whosoever believed
> In him should not perish, but have everlasting life
> John 3:16

Here, the manifestation of the love of God for the sinful world is seen in how he gave up his only begotten Son as a sacrificial Lamb to take away the sins of the world (John 1:29,36; Revelation 5:6-14; 1Peter 2:24). This was to bring about God's salvation unto mankind.

And this manifestation of his love has to do with allowing his only begotten and beloved Son Jesus Christ to go through suffering and pain to die the death of the cross; something which the bible reveals he had purposed in himself even before the world began. In sharing a light on the manifested love of God for mankind, the bible says;

> In this was manifested the love of God Toward us,
> Because that God sent his only Begotten Son into the world
> That we might live through him
> Herein is love, not that we loved God but that
> He loved us and sent his Son to be the
> Propitiation for our sins
> 1John 4:9-10

By the works of the cross of Christ, God also revealed and tangibly demonstrated the depths and extensions of his love, not only to the world but also for the world. It is true that this kind of love can never be understood by the human mind. It can only take God's revealed and imparted knowledge by his Holy Spirit to actually grasp it. The apostle Paul who had a revelation of God's love in his prayer for the church in Ephesus prayed;

> That Christ may dwell in your hearts
> By faith; that ye being rooted and grounded
> In love may be able to comprehend with all saints
> What is the breath and length and depth and height
> And to know the love of Christ which passeth knowledge
> That ye might be filled with all the fullness of God
> Ephesians 3:17-19

You see, knowledge of the love of God in and through Christ is very important for us to be filled with the fullness of God whose temple we are (1Corinthians 3:16). And as the temple of God, we are supposed to be filled with God in his fullness by having Christ in us, who is the embodiment of the Godhead (Colossians 2:9-10). Not only that, we are also to be filled with the abundance and overflow of all that he is and all that he has for us in Christ. Amen. Christ Jesus said unto us;

> The thief cometh not, but for to steal,
> And to kill, and to destroy: I am come that they might
> Have life, and that they might have it more abundantly.
> John 10:10

One day I was sharing about the love of God with a Muslim friend. He was very attentive but with a mixture of curiosity. At a certain point he cut across the conversation to ask whether it was possible for man to love the way God loves us which I answered him in the affirmative. When he heard the answer in the affirmative, he exclaimed and said; "no it is impossible!" And when he said that, I could understand his point of view so I stopped dragging our nice conversation into an argument. However, I made him to understand why it was possible from the biblical point of view. The truth is that we can love just as God loves because God has made it possible for us in Jesus Christ by his Spirit that dwells in us. It should also be known that only the love of God or a love which only comes from God is operated by his Holy Spirit. Without the Holy Spirit, the love of God cannot be operated in and through a person. The bible reveals that God has indeed given us of his love (Romans 5:5) by which we are supposed to love one another (John 15:12). Again the bible says that, manifesting the love of God is an indication of his dwelling presence in us as we read;

> Hereby perceive we the love of God
> Because he laid down his life for us
> We ought to lay down our lives for the brethren
> 1John 3:16

> Beloved, if God so loved us we ought also to
> Love one another. No man hath seen God at anytime
> If we love one another, God dwelleth in us
> And his love is perfected in us.
> 1John 4:11-12

Here, the bible states clearly that it is his (God's) love that is in us and which is supposed to be perfected in and through us. It is not our own love and therefore cannot be perfected in our own way. But the perfection of God's love in us and through us is only made possible by God's own Holy Spirit. He is the inspiration and worker of all and everything which God has placed in us in Christ; and that includes his love. In talking about the love of God in us, the bible says;

> And hope maketh not ashamed
> Because the love of God is shed abroad
> In our hearts by the Holy Ghost
> Which is given unto us
> Romans 5:5

> But we have this treasure (of God's love) in earthen vessels
> That the excellency of the power may be of God
> And not of us
> 2 Corinthians 4: 7

> For it is God which worketh in you (us)
> Both to will and to do of his good pleasure
> Philippians 3:12

And by working for us to will and do of his good pleasure, and for this matter his love in and through us, God causes us to multiply, increase and abound more and more into the overflow of his love (Ephesians 3:20). In the abundance and overflow of God's love, it becomes necessarily possible to love even them that hate us and are enemies to us. The Lord Jesus Christ revealed the possibility of God's love working in and through us when he taught us this way;

> Ye have heard that it hath been said,
> Thou shalt love thy neighbour, and hate thine enemy.
> But I say unto you, Love your enemies, bless them that curse you,
> Do good to them that hate you, and pray for

them which despitefully use you,
And persecute you; that ye may be the children of your Father
Which is in heaven: for he maketh his sun to
rise on the evil and on the good,
And sendeth rain on the just and on the unjust; for if ye love them
Which love you, what reward have ye? Do not even
The publicans the same?
Matthew 5:43-48

Then again the apostle Paul in a similar way to encourage the Church or the Body of Christ added;

If it be possible, as much as lieth in you,
Live peaceably with all men. Dearly beloved,
Avenge not yourselves, but rather give place unto wrath:
For it is written, Vengeance is mine; I will repay, saith the Lord.
Therefore if thine enemy hunger, feed him; if he thirst,
Give him drink: for in so doing thou shalt heap coals
Of fire on his head; be not overcome of evil,
But overcome evil with good.
Romans 12:18-21

In his prayers for the churches, the apostle Paul could always be heard praying that their love for one another would grow, increase and abound. For the Philippians Church he prayed;

And this I pray that your love
May abound yet more and more in knowledge
And in all judgment; that ye may approve things
That are excellent; that ye may be sincere
And without offence till the day of Christ
Philippians 1:9
(Ephesians 1:3-4)

For the Thessalonians Church, the apostle prayed;

And the Lord make you to increase
And abound in love one toward another
And toward all men, even as we do toward you;
To the end he may stablish your hearts unblameable in holiness
Before God even our Father at the coming of our
Lord Jesus Christ with all his saints
1Thessalonians 3:12

And then again he prays;

We are bound to thank God always for you, Brethren
As it is meet, because that your faith groweth exceedingly
And the charity (love) of every one of you all
Toward each other aboundeth
2Thessalonians 1:3

Love for one another and also for all men is one of the strong foundations of the Christian faith; for the bible says;

For in Jesus Christ neither circumcision
Availeth any thing, nor uncircumcision;
But faith which worketh by love
Galatians 5:6

Now we have the commandment from our Lord Jesus Christ to love one another, even just as he loved and gave himself unto us. The Lord Jesus told us;

This is my commandment,
That ye love one another, as I have loved you
Greater love hath no man than this, that a man
Lay down his life for his friends.
John 15:12-13

And then our Lord goes on to add why it is so important to him for us to love one another as he loved and still loves us;

> A new commandment I give unto you,
> That ye love one another; as I have loved you,
> That ye also love one another; by this shall all men
> Know that ye are my disciples, if ye
> Have love one to another
> John 13:34-35

If it were not possible, I don't believe he would have asked us to do so; because God as our Father in heaven would not ask us to do anything which he knows he has not equipped us for in Christ. By this we can also declare with the apostle Paul;

> I can do all things through Christ which strengtheneth me.
> Philippians 4:13

> Jesus said unto him,
> If thou canst believe, all things are possible
> To him that believeth.
> Mark 9:23

Like the apostle Paul, what we need to do in these last days for one another in Christ is to be praying for the love of God among the body of Christ to grow, increase and abound. If the early church understood and lived to abound in the love of God, we also in these end times should count it important and make it a priority in our lives where we are constantly praying for one another to abound in the love of God. We are even encouraged to provoke ourselves unto the love for one another as we see the day of the Lord's coming and approaching (Hebrews 10:24-25).

It should not be so strange for us to understand why all these prayers and the provoking of one another to abound in the love of God should be made for one another in the body of Christ. Apart from it being a sign of unity in the body of Christ for the world to know and see that we are his disciples; I also believe it to be a means and a part of being awake for the Lord's coming as he cautioned us concerning things that would happen before his coming. He said;

> And then shall many be offended and shall
> Betray one another… and because iniquity shall abound
> The love of many shall wax cold but he that shall endure
> Unto the end the same shall be saved
> Matthew 24:10, 12-13

And the love of the many that shall wax cold refers to the love of God which is in the believer. This is not the moment to relax in our love for God, our neighbours and for one another in the body of Christ.

THE NATURE OF GOD'S LOVE

So great and powerful is the love of God that, not even the sins of mankind could cause it to stop flowing. The bible says that God is love (1John 4:8) and that, his love for us is great (Ephesians 2:4) which was he manifested and demonstrated in the truth that, while we were yet sinners, he made Christ to come and die for us (Romans 5:8)

Such a love is supernatural and goes beyond the understanding of the human mind; and if we can understand and walk in such a love, we would overcome many things in our daily lives in terms of relations. Whatever God is, so is his love and whatever the love of God is, so also is God himself. If God is kind, so also is his love. If God is faithful, so also is his love. If God is great, so also is his love.

The bible says that our God, who is love, is also a consuming fire (Hebrews 12:29). And being a consuming fire, his love is also consuming as fire. It is written that the vehemence of the flame of God's love cannot be quenched by any amount of water (Song of Solomon 8:6-7). In other words the love of God as fire consumes every form of hatred, jealousy, malice and bitterness of the heart. Nothing can in no way overcome the love of God. God's love is the refiner of the heart and I personally believe it also to be a divine medication of healing to all forms of emotional heart and mind diseases. The love of God is applied in our lives by faith with action in his word (Proverbs 4:20-22).

I stand to be corrected but I believe it is the consuming aspect of God's love that covered the sins of man for him to be able to forgive the sins of man, give and send his only begotten Son to come, offer himself and suffer to die for the sins of the world.

Sin cannot stop God's love for a person but by his love; and in and through his love, sin can be overcome. The truth is that, sin has already been overcome by the love of God which he manifested through the sacrifice of his only begotten Son Jesus Christ on the cross (1John 4:10). Let us hear some of what the bible says concerning this;

> Hatred stirreth up strifes, but love covereth all sins
> Proverbs 10:12

> Wherefore I say unto thee,
> Her sins, which are many, are forgiven;
> For she loved much:
> But to whom little is forgiven,
> The same loveth little.
> Luke 7:47

> For God so loved the world,
> That he gave his only begotten Son,
> That whosoever believeth in him should not perish,
> But have everlasting life.
> John 3:16

> But God commendeth his love toward us,
> In that, while we were yet sinners,
> Christ died for us.
> Romans 5:8

The apostle Paul in spite of all he did to persecute the Body of Christ later came to know, understand and embrace that wonderful love of God unto which he attributed the existence of his life. He boldly declared;

> I am crucified with Christ: nevertheless I live;
> Yet not I, but Christ liveth in me: and the life which I now live
> In the flesh, I live by the faith of the Son of God,
> Who loved me, and gave himself for me.
> Galatians 2:20;

Then the apostle John in the book of Revelation puts it this way;

> And from Jesus Christ,
> Who is the faithful witness, and the first begotten
> Of the dead, and the prince of the kings of the earth
> Unto him that loved us, and washed us
> From our sins in his own blood,
> Revelation 1:5

The love here that covers all sins refers to the love of God; and how does love and for that matter the love of God covers all sins? It is because of the vehemence of its unquenchable flame which also shapes to give it a character. A character that is able to subdue every works of the flesh, sin and evil. Again let us hear what the bible teaches to reveal about the love of God to us;

> Charity (love) suffereth long and is kind
> Charity envieth not, charity vaunteth not itself
> Is not puffed up, doth not behave itself unseemly
> Seeketh not her own, is not easily provoked
> Thinketh no evil, rejoiceth not in iniquity
> But rejoiceth in the truth
> 1Corinthians 13:4-6

It is the characteristic of what the love of God is made that makes it divinely able to forgive and possibly forget the sins of man. In the establishment of the New Covenant God said;

> For I will be merciful to their unrighteousness,
> And their sins and their iniquities will I

> Remember no more.
> Hebrews 8:12

King David by the inspiration of the Holy Spirit declared it this way;

> Blessed is the man
> Unto whom the Lord imputeth not iniquity,
> And in whose spirit there is no guile.
> Psalm 32:2

And the apostle Paul elaborating on the love and forgiveness of God put it this way;

> To wit, that God was in Christ,
> Reconciling the world unto himself, not imputing
> Their trespasses unto them; and hath committed
> Unto us the word of reconciliation
> 2 Corinthians 5:19

Though the love of God could face, encounter and go through sufferings and envies of all sorts; it has an over winning, overcoming and a more than a conquering nature with a consuming vehemence or force of flame which, nothing of a situation or a circumstance whatsoever is able to overcome it (Song of Solomon 8:6-7). Neither should we as believers in Christ allow anything to separate us from the love of God (Romans 8:37-39); because it is the kind of love in Christ that is able to constrain the believer (2Corinthians 5:13-14) to first love God with all his heart, soul and mind (Matthew 22:37) and hold on to the word and promises of God by faith till he or she has seen results (John 14:15).

The love of God is also the kind of love which constrains the believer to be able to love his neighbour as him or herself (Matthew 22:38; Luke 10:27) and even an enemy (Matthew 5:43-45). It is the kind of love that enables the believer in Christ to love one another in the body of Christ (John 13:34-35; John 15:12,17; Romans 13:8;

1John 3:11,23; Galatians 5:13; Ephesians 4:2; 1Thessalonians 3:12; 1Thessalonians 4:9; Hebrews 10:24; 1Peter 1:22; 1Peter 3:8; 1John 4:7-8,11-12; 2John 1:5-6).

And it is the only kind of love that enables the believer in Jesus Christ to love without fear (2Timothy 1:7; 1John 4:18) and dissimulation (Romans 12:9-10; 1Timothy 1:5), but in deed and in truth (1John 3:17-18)

Lack of these divine abilities to love God, your neighbour and one another within the body of Christ is a sign of not having the love of God in a person (John 5:42); or that one's love of God is rather growing cold (Matthew 24:10- 13). And lack of the love of God for one another is the absence of eternal life in a person. Eternal life in Jesus Christ is only manifested, experienced, demonstrated and fulfilled in and through the love of God that abides in us (Galatians 5:6: Ephesians 1:4-7).

You see, eternal life means you live forever. Eternal life means passage or a translation from death unto life in Christ Jesus; and it is always in connection with the love of God. When we love God we believe in him and his word. Jesus said;

> If ye love me, keep my commandments.
> John 14:15

> Verily, verily, I say unto you,
> He that heareth my word, and believeth on him
> That sent me, hath everlasting life, and shall not come
> Into condemnation; but is passed from death unto life.
> John 5:24
> (John 3:16)

This is how the bible reveals eternal life in connection with the love of God in us for one another;

> We know that we have passed from
> Death to life because we love the brethren,
> He that loveth not his brother abideth in death,

> Whosoever hateth his brother is a murderer
> And ye know that no murderer hath
> Eternal life abiding in him
> 1John 3:14-16
> (John 17:3)

It is good to know that the power of the love of God can in no way be underestimated; because it is the only kind of love that is able to bear all things, believe all things, hope all things and endure all things by faith in the promises of God since it never fails (1Corinthians 13:7-8).

It has the power to do what the word of God says since it is purposed to keep the word of God. You see, by the love of God the believer in Jesus Christ is able to endure and persevere with patience as he or she journeys by faith through eternal life on earth in this world; a world in which he or she is, but not of (John 17:14)

The good news is that, love is the manifestation of God in the fullness of his power and glory on earth and in this world seen in and through the believer in Christ (1John 4:8, 12). It is also the Father's plan and purpose, as well as his good and successful end for us as his children, that we should live and walk in love (Ephesians 1:1-2)

This is in order for us to manifest the fullness of his glory and his power out of his kingdom on earth in and through his love (John 17:22-23). It is also in order for us to reign and to rule in life on earth and in this world (Romans 5:17).

This is exactly the purpose of God concerning the cross of Christ and all that happened with it, on it and around it in relations with his love for mankind. Hallelujah.

Something to know; God by his great love and mercy loved us to give and send his only begotten Son Jesus Christ. Jesus Christ the only begotten and beloved Son of God came to manifest this love unto mankind through his life and death on the cross. By his Holy Spirit, the bible says that God has imparted this same love of his into our hearts.

Dear born again believer in Christ, what are you doing with such great treasure? Be blessed in his name.

CHAPTER TWO

BEFORE THE CROSS

• •

BEFORE OUR LORD JESUS Christ went to the cross, the bible says that he came out of his glory to live among us on earth, and in this world. And it was not a perfect world that he came into. Rather it was a world of sin and full of darkness. It was a world that has fallen from the glory of God and therefore knew not God or willing to have anything to do with God.

But when for his great love with which he still loved this world of darkness got manifested, God gave unto the world his only begotten Son. And when God gave his only beloved and begotten Son, he did not keep his Son Jesus Christ in heaven. He sent him down to the earth into this world to serve and fulfill the purpose for which he gave his Son. So the only beloved and begotten Son of the living God came to be and live with us. God gave him, God sent him and therefore, Jesus came.

This is important for us to know that Jesus Christ did not come by himself, but that he was sent by God. Yes, He was sent by the Father. And also that God sent him into this world for a purpose. It is also important to know this in order to divinely understand the Lord Jesus Christ and to know him in consideration to how he lived, said and did what he said and did while he walked on the face of this earth and in this world. It is also more important to know this in order to understand why the Lord Jesus Christ faced and went through some of the things he faced and went through in connection with his life and even death on the cross. Another important thing is to know and understand what all these have to do in relation to mankind but especially to you who by a divine appointment are reading this book.

The bible reveals that Christ in coming into the world came and manifested in the form of man. Truly, it was in the form of man that he came to fulfill the divine purposes of God. The word of God makes us to understand that, he did not come in the form of an angel or any other heavenly being to fulfill God's purpose concerning mankind which was to save them through his death on the cross; a death which opened the way for man to reconcile again unto God (2Corinthians 5:18-20).

Being the only beloved and the only begotten One, the bible says that it is by him, with him, through him and for him that God the Father had created all things. Here are some few scriptures that help to throw some light on it;

> In the beginning was the Word,
> And the Word was with God, and the Word was God.
> The same was in the beginning with God. All things were made
> By him; and without him was not anything made that was made
> John 1:1-3

> For by him were all things created,
> That are in heaven, and that are in earth, visible and
> Invisible, whether they be thrones, or dominions,
> Or principalities, or powers: all things were
> Created by him, and for him:
> Colossians 1:16

And this Son of the living God as the Word by whom, with whom, through whom and for whom all things were made, came to dwell among us in a human form or as a form of man. The bible records in the book of John;

> And the word was made flesh and dwelt among us
> (And we beheld his glory, the glory as of the only
> Begotten of the Father), full of grace and truth
> John 1:1-3, 14

Again the bible says that the Son of God did not come in the fullness of his glory. He left all his glory and all his attributes to become poor as the fallen man by taking upon himself the humble nature of a servant in order to do and fulfill the Father's purpose.

However, Christ Jesus did not live anyhow. He lived in the knowledge of not only who and what he was; but also in the knowledge of where he came from, the purpose of why he came and where he was going to go. This divine strategy of knowing helped to propel him unto the success and the victory he won over Satan

CHRIST JESUS KNEW WHERE HE CAME FROM . . .

Throughout his life on the face of this earth and in this world, Jesus Christ, Son of the living God always knew where he came from. He knew that he had from heaven above. He knew that he had come from the Father in heaven. And he knew that the Father had sent him into the world as the second Adam and the promised seed that will bruise the head of Satan.

> The first man is of the earth, earthy:
> The second man is the Lord from heaven.
> 1Corinthians 15:47

The first man which is of the earth and therefore earthy refers to Adam. He was the first man and the bible reveals that God created and made him in his image and likeness by first forming him from the dust of the ground. After forming him from the dust of the ground, the bible says that God breathed into him the breadth of life which made him to become a living soul.

The second man which is the Lord from heaven is referring to the Lord Jesus Christ. He was not created, made or formed like the first man Adam; but as the Word and the Son of the living God, he was in the beginning with God and was God in heaven from where he was sent into the world. No wonder Christ Jesus was able to boldly declare to the Jews concerning himself;

> For I came down from heaven,
> Not to do mine own will, but the will of him that sent me…
> They said, "Is not this Jesus, the son of Joseph,
> Whose father and mother we know? How does he now say,
> 'I have come down from heaven'?"
> John 6:38, 42

It is said that "Knowledge is Power"; and this cannot be far from the truth. Knowing from where he came gave our Lord the divine ability not to bother himself of whether the Jews believed him or not. The way and how they thought they knew him in the natural sense couldn't change his mind of where he knew he came from. This could be an example for us as his followers too. We as his followers can and must learn to identify ourselves with the source of who, what and where the word of God says we are and from.

We are of the kingdom of God in the world but not of the word (John 17:16). This makes us the citizens of God's kingdom on earth. Something we should hold on to in reality by faith in a way that, no matter what people may say or do; we remain unshakable by the source of where we know that we are from. We are born of God (John 1:12-13) and therefore are the children of God. Hallelujah!

Knowing where he came from; the Lord Jesus Christ said to Nicodemus;

> And no man hath ascended up to heaven,
> But he that came down from heaven,
> Even the Son of man which is in heaven
> John 3:13

And then once in a question form, he threw some light on where he knew he came from when he said to the disciples;

> Then what if you were to see the Son of Man
> Ascending to where he was before?
> John 6:62

Again in a discussion with the Jews in the temple; the lord said to reveal the source of where he came from;

> And he said unto them,
> Ye are from beneath; I am from above:
> Ye are of this world; I am not of this world.
> John 8:23

God the Father also used John the Baptist who was sent to prepare the way for the Lord's coming to confirm his heavenly origin. So in his testimony concerning Jesus Christ, John the Baptist also confirmed it this way;

> He that cometh from above is above all:
> He that is of the earth is earthly, and speaketh of the earth:
> He that cometh from heaven is above all.
> John 3:31

Coming from heaven above, the Lord Jesus Christ also spoke of the things that were of heaven above. He said to Nicodemus in a conversation with him;

> Verily, verily, I say unto thee,
> We speak that we do know, and testify that we have seen;
> And ye receive not our witness. If I have told you earthly things,
> And ye believe not, how shall ye believe,
> If I tell you of heavenly things?
> John 3:11-12

CHRIST JESUS KNEW WHO HE WAS . . .

Throughout his life on the face of this earth and in this world, Jesus Christ, Son of the living God always knew who he was. Jesus Christ knew he was the Son of God and therefore lived also to comport himself as a Son of God. The bible records;

> For God so loved the world,
> That he gave his only begotten Son, that whosoever
> Believeth in him should not perish, but have everlasting life.
> John 3:16

The Father bore witness to confirm this knowledge while Christ Jesus was on the earth. Once during his baptism by John the Baptist, (Matthew 3:16- 17); and then again on what is usually known as the mount of transfiguration (Mathew 17:1-5). In both of these places the Father declared to confirm the son ship of Christ when he said, "This is my beloved Son."

And as a Son, he knew that he was one with the Father;

> I and the Father are one."
> John 10:30

> And now I am no more in the world,
> But these are in the world, and I come to thee.
> Holy Father, keep through thine own name those
> Whom thou hast given me that they may be one, as we are
> John 17:11

> And the glory which thou gavest me
> I have given them; that they may be one,
> Even as we are one:
> John 17:22

> If ye had known me,
> Ye should have known my Father also:
> And from henceforth ye know him, and have seen him.
> John 14:7

Being one with the Father, there is none other person in and through whom any person in heaven, on earth or under the earth could ever get to the Father. And likewise, as the Lord Jesus pointed unto us when he walked on the face of the earth; none other person can come to him except the Father draws him unto the Son.

> Jesus therefore answered and said unto them,
> Murmur not among yourselves. No man can come to me,
> Except the Father which hath sent me draw him:
> And I will raise him up at the last day.
> John 6:43-44

> Jesus saith unto him,
> I am the way, the truth, and the life:
> No man cometh unto the Father, but by me.
> John 14:6

Jesus Christ as the Way… The one and only narrow but safe way to the Father in Heaven

- Hebrews 9:8-15
- Hebrews 10:19-22
- Hebrews 4:15-16
- Ephesians 2:12-18
- Colossians 1:16-22
- 1Timothy 2:5-6
- Matthew 20:28
- John 10:9-10
- Matthew 7:13-14

Jesus Christ as the Truth… The one and only Truth that is able to set mankind free of all bondages.

- John 1:1-2
- John 1:14
- John 1:16-17
- John 18:37
- Matthew 22:16
- John 8:40

John 8:31-32, 37
2John 1:1-2
1John 5:20

Jesus Christ as the Life… The one and the only life of God that makes a person live forever or eternally in glory.

John 5:25-26
John 1:4
1John 1:1-2
John 11:25-26
John 6:57-58
1John 5:11-12
John 6:68 (John 17:8; John 12:48-50; Acts 5:20)
John 3:16
John 10:27-29
John 17:1-3
Colossians 3:3-4 (Galatians 2:20)
1Corinthians 6:17
2Corinthians 3:17-18 (Colossians 1:27; John 17:22-24)

CHRIST JESUS KNEW WHY HE CAME…

> He that committeth sin is of the devil;
> For the devil sinneth from the beginning.
> For this purpose the Son of God was manifested,
> That he might destroy the works of the devil.
> 1John 3:8

Throughout his life on the face of this earth and in this world, Jesus Christ, Son of the living God always knew why he came on earth in this world. He knew he had come to do the Father's will. And the Father's will for him was to take away the sins of mankind, save and deliver them from the bondage of Satan and restore man back into relationship with the father by the shedding of his blood as a sacrificial lamb. This is what the bible says;

> For it was not possible that the blood of bulls and of
> Goats should take away sins, wherefore when he cometh
> Into the world, he saith, sacrifice and offering thou wouldest not
> But a body hast thou prepared me, in burnt offering and
> Sacrifices for sin thou hast had no pleasure;
> Then said I, Lo, I come (in the volume of the book it is
> Written of me) to do thy will, O God
> Hebrews 10:4-7

He said unto the Jews;

> For I came down from heaven not to do
> My own will, but the will of him that sent me
> John 6:38

And then to his disciples, he said;

> Jesus said unto them
> My meat is to do the will of him that sent me
> And to finish his work
> John 4:34

It took the spirit of humility for Jesus Christ to submit himself in every area of his life on earth in order for the will of the Father to come to pass. The bible reveals him to be submissive even to his natural parents of Joseph and Mary. This was after they went to Jerusalem with Jesus as young boy where they lost contact with the boy Jesus but later on found him in the midst of the great teachers of the Torah;

> And he said unto them,
> How is it that ye sought me? Wist ye not
> That I must be about my Father's business?
> And they understood not the saying which

> He spake unto them. And he went down with them,
> And came to Nazareth, and was subject unto them:
> But his mother kept all these sayings in her heart.
> Luke 2:49-51

Even his coming for John the Baptist to baptize him in the Jordan River is in itself a sign of humility considering what John testified about Jesus and his shoes;

> I indeed baptize you with water unto repentance:
> But he that cometh after me is mightier than I, whose shoes
> I am not worthy to bear: he shall baptize you with the Holy Ghost,
> And with fire: Whose fan is in his hand, and he will
> Throughly purge his floor, and gather his wheat
> Into the garner; but he will burn up the chaff
> With unquenchable fire
> Matthew 3:11-12

All these were for the sake of the Father's will.

> Then cometh Jesus from Galilee to Jordan
> Unto John, to be baptized of him But John forbad him,
> Saying, I have need to be baptized of thee, and comest thou to me?
> And Jesus answering said unto him, suffer it to be so now:
> For thus it becometh us to fulfill all righteousness.
> Matthew 3:13-15

Whiles in the world, the bible reveals Jesus Christ was in the form of God but he did not think it robbery to be equal with God; but for the sake of humility, meekness and humbleness, he took upon himself the form of a servant and was made in the likeness of men (Philippians 2:6-7). The bible also says that Christ in leaving behind all his glory to come into this world, did not put on the nature of angels but took on him the seed of Abraham. In other words, he took on the human body of flesh and blood (Hebrews 2:16; Galatians 3:13-14, 16). It was in this human form that Jesus Christ manifested to live among us; and it was in this human form that Jesus Christ learnt obedience and humility while he pursued the Father's will. The bible records;

> And being found in fashion as a man
> He humbled himself and became obedient
> Unto death, even the death of the cross
> Philippians 2:8

In his humility, God also exalted and gave him a name that is above every other name (Philippians 2:9-10). Here, we can understand and learn by revelation that just as pride comes before a fall; so does humility and humbleness comes before exaltation. The apostle Peter reminds us this way in his epistles;

> Humble yourselves therefore
> Under the mighty hand of God,
> That he may exalt you in due time:
> 1Peter 5:6

And the apostle James also in his epistle declared;

> But he giveth more grace.
> Wherefore he saith, God resisteth the proud,
> But giveth grace unto the humble.
> James 4:6

> Humble yourselves
> In the sight of the Lord, and he shall lift you up.
> James 4:10

However, humbleness involves being obedient to hear, do and walk in the will, the ways, the plans and the purposes of God in life. It is one of the ways of the kingdom that Jesus Christ came to teach us by how he lived on the earth through his words and actions. He said unto us;

Take my yoke upon you
And learn of me, for I am meek and lowly
In heart, and ye shall find rest unto your souls
Matthew 11:29

LEARNING FROM THE MASTER...

Being humble plays an important role in our relationship with God. It leads us into the rest of God. If our Lord Jesus Christ humbled himself unto the Father when he came into the world as a man, I believe it is also a lesson for us who are already in the world to learn to be humble unto our Father who is in heaven and whose name needs to be hallowed (Matthew 6:9). It is him alone who also needs to be worshipped (Matthew 4:10).

The bible says that God resists the proud, but he gives grace to the humble (James 4:6) and that we should humble ourselves in the sight of the Lord, and he shall lift us up (James 4:10).

If it is the humble that is given and receives grace, then going to the Father before the throne to obtain mercy and find grace, should also be in the spirit of meekness and humbleness as the word of God reveals;

Let us therefore come boldly
Unto the throne of grace, that we may obtain mercy,
And find grace to help in time of need.
Hebrews 4:16

Many may not be aware but humbleness, meekness and lowliness or humility as the Christian's way of life in Christ is a sign of faith, trust and confidence in the Lord. In fact, they are signs of divine boldness, courage and strength in the life of the righteous to take bold steps of faith in doing the things of God in his will, plans and purposes. Let me share a mystery with you.

The bible says that the righteous is as bold as a lion (Proverbs 28:1). However, every time we hear of a lion, we should learn to set our minds on the Lion of the tribe of Judah and not on the physical animal lion as we humanly know; especially in the mystery which I want to share with you. Neither should we think of the demonic lion who is roaring to find whom he may devour (1Peter 5:8). It is good and encouraging to know that it is by the righteousness of Jesus Christ who himself is the Lion of the tribe of Judah that we also have been made righteous (2Corinthians 5:21).

If that is the case and I faithfully believe it to be so; then our boldness is likened to his boldness just as his righteousness also makes us righteous. Therefore the boldness of the righteous is as the boldness of the Lion of the tribe of Judah who prevailed to take the scroll from the hand of him that sat upon the throne. And having received the righteousness of God, we have also received the divine ability to be bold and courageous. How? In and through him by whose righteousness we have been made righteous as kings and priests to reign and to rule in life (Romans 5:17)

This is a divine boldness which embodies humbleness, meekness and lowliness or humility in heart to pursue the righteousness of God. It is his righteousness that enables us to overcome as his Church without being prevailed over by the gates of Hades (Matthew 16:18; Matthew 7:13-14), but to possess the gate of the enemy (Genesis 22:17) to trample over the enemy and all his power (Luke 10:19).

King David in one of his Psalms declared "...yea though I walk through the valley of the shadow of death, I will fear no evil for thou art with me"; and one of the reasons is that; "he leads me in the path of righteousness" (Psalm 23:1-6)

It is the righteousness of God that humbles the Believer, but it is also the righteousness of God that empowers him to prevail and to rule (Romans 5:17). Humbleness is that which make us bold to submit and be committed to the things of God by way of his will, plans and purposes just like Jesus Christ (Philippians 2:5-8)

See, when the apostle John was told not to weep because the lion of the tribe of Judah has prevailed to take the scroll upon which no man in heaven, on earth or under the earth even dared to look upon from the hand of him that sat upon the throne; he was later shown the image of the Lion of the tribe of Judah to be a lamb that had been slain (Revelation 5:1-13).

No wonder the bible says that when the lion of the tribe of Judah manifested and came in the form of man, he humbled himself and was bold even unto the death on the cross (Philippians 2:5-8). But the prophet Isaiah put it this way concerning the Lord's humbleness as a sign of boldness to face death on the cross in order to fulfill God's plan for mankind;

> He was oppressed and he was afflicted
> Yet he opened not his mouth
> He is brought as a lamb to the slaughter
> And as a sheep before her shearers is dumb
> So he openeth not his mouth
> Isaiah 53:7

The apostle Peter also said concerning the Lord Jesus Christ in his humbleness to have the will of God done as this;

> Who did no sin, neither was guile found
> In his mouth; who when reviled, reviled not again
> When he suffered, he threatened not, but committed
> Himself to him that judgeth righteously
> 1Peter 2:22-2

And the Lord said of himself unto the disciples;

> Therefore doth my Father love me
> Because I lay down my life that I might take it again
> No man taketh it from me, but I lay it down of myself
> I have power to lay it down, and I have power
> To take it again, this commandment
> Have I received of my Father
> John 10:17-18

In talking about what and how we can go boldly before the Lord at the throne in a way that could please him, the prophet Micah reveals a little bit of God's heart to us in terms of humbleness when he said;

> He hath shown thee O man what is good
> And what doth the Lord require of thee
> But to do justly and to love mercy and to
> Walk humbly with thy God?
> Micah 6:6-8

So we can learn from how the Lord Jesus Christ lived in the spirit of meekness and humbleness by submitting to both his earthly parents on earth and his heavenly Father (Luke 2:51).

Suffering and death for Christ in the flesh was inevitable; therefore it was good and necessary for Christ to manifest and come in the human form. This was in order to taste of how it really is like to be in the fallen state of man and to feel their infirmities. By this, God's plan of salvation could be fulfilled and be perfected. The suffering of Christ was the Father's own way of drawing more sons into his glory; and therefore prepared a body for him (Hebrews 10:5). It was a body prepared and made to bear all form of sufferings and every bit of the curses man incurred through the sins of Adam. By that body, God the Father had planned for him to suffer and taste of death for all mankind. The word of God records it like this;

> But we see Jesus who was made a little
> Lower than the angels for the suffering of death
> Crowned with glory and honour; that he by the grace of God
> Should taste of death for every man, for it became him
> For who are all things, and by whom are all things
> In bringing many sons unto glory, to make
> The captain of their salvation perfect
> Through sufferings
> Hebrews 2:9-10

Not only was he to taste of death for everyman; but by that death, he also could destroy him that had the power of death which is the devil; and deliver man from the bondage of death (Hebrews 2:14-15)

It was also a body prepared and made to bear all the pain, grieves, weaknesses, and infirmities of all iniquities, sins, sicknesses and diseases of mankind. So the word of God concerning Christ Jesus says;

> Who his own self
> Bare our sins in his own body on the tree,
> That we, being dead to sins, should live unto righteousness:
> By whose stripes ye were healed.
> 1Peter 2:24
> (Isaiah 53:4; Matthew 8:17; Matthew 4:23; Matthew 9:35; Hebrews 9:28)

So out of his glory, Christ the only begotten Son of the living God came into the world where he manifested with a human body in the personality of Jesus Christ. It was the will of God that while Jesus Christ was in the human form, the world would know, recognize and acknowledge him as his true Son. About two times God spoke and said concerning Jesus Christ;

> ...This is my beloved Son
> In whom I am well pleased
> Matthew 4:17

This was the first time God the Father spoke concerning Jesus Christ to reveal the mystery of Jesus as his Son. It was during the time when John the Baptist baptized Jesus in the river Jordan. Then the second time was when Jesus got transfigured on the mountain with the inner circle of the three disciples Peter, James and John. There the Father spoke and said;

> ...This is my beloved Son
> In whom I am well pleased
> Hear ye him
> Matthew 17:5

Then again as if the Master wanted to make sure that the people which the Father had given unto him (John 17:6); and whom he had chosen to be with him wherever he went have actually come to know him after sometime of being together with him. So he asked them; ". . . who do men say that I the Son of man am?" (Matthew 16:13). It was after they had struggled about what and how others say and think about Jesus that he put forth the direct question to the disciples as to whom they the disciples know and see him to be. And by revelation, one of them named Peter declared;

> And Simon Peter answered and said
> Thou art the Christ, the Son of the living God
> Matthew 16:16

God sent Jesus Christ to the world that we may see him, know him, accept him, receive him and believe in him to be who and what he is; Son of the most high God; the Messiah and the Saviour of the world. Hence;

> For God so loved the world,
> That he gave his only begotten Son, that whosoever believeth
> In him should not perish, but have everlasting life.
> For God sent not his Son into the world
> To condemn the world; but that the world
> Through him might be saved.
> John 3:16-17

CHRIST JESUS KNEW WHERE HE WAS GOING . . .

Throughout his life on the face of this earth and in this world, Jesus Christ, Son of the living God always knew where he was going. Here the bible by many scriptures show to reveal how Christ Jesus lived and walked in complete knowledge of where he was going and its timing;

> Now before the feast of the Passover,
> When Jesus knew that his hour was come that he should
> Depart out of this world unto the Father,

> Having loved his own which were in the world,
> He loved them unto the end.
> John 13:1

> Jesus knowing that the Father had given
> All things into his hands, and that he was come
> From God, and went to God...
> John 13:3

In a discussion with his disciples he spoke and said unto them;

> I came forth from the Father, and am come into the world:
> Again, I leave the world, and go to the Father.
> John 16:28

> Verily, verily, I say unto you,
> He that believeth on me, the works that I do shall he do also;
> And greater works than these shall he do;
> Because I go unto my Father
> John 14:12

> Ye have heard how I said unto you, I go away,
> And come again unto you. If ye loved me,
> Ye would rejoice, because I said, I go unto the Father:
> For my Father is greater than I.
> John 14:28

CHRIST JESUS LIVED IN CONSTANT COMMUNION WITH THE FATHER . . .

Throughout his life on the face of this earth and in this world, Jesus Christ, Son of the living God always lived in constant communion with his heavenly Father. This constant communion with the Father was exercised or made possible through prayer. Prayer simply means conversation or communication with God as a Father in heaven; not as a father on earth. Neither is it to a God of a distant, but a God with whom you have a personal intimate relationship as your source of everything in life. Jesus taught us;

> But thou, when thou prayest,
> Enter into thy closet, and when thou hast shut thy door,
> Pray to thy Father which is in secret; and thy Father which
> Seeth in secret shall reward thee openly.
> Matthew 6:6

> After this manner therefore pray ye:
> Our Father which art in heaven, Hallowed be thy name.
> Matthew 6:9

And prayer was the means by which the Son reached out spiritually to the Father in Heaven. In the same and similar way the Father also reached down to the Son on earth. As an example for us, we as the Lord's followers can maintain a constant communion with God as our Father in heaven through prayer. Father simply means Source and giver of life. Its meaning also includes a provider and one that you depend upon. In consideration of all these with God as our Father, Source and provider upon whom we depend, a constant communion or communication with him becomes vital hence prayer.

THE MASTER'S PRAYER LIFE

Prayer was a lifestyle of our Lord Jesus Christ when he lived among men on earth. Even till he gave up the spirit on the cross he was in prayer. During the time of his baptism, the Lord was in communion with the Father praying;

> Now when all the people were baptized,
> It came to pass, that Jesus also being baptized,
> And praying, the heaven was opened,
> Luke 3:21

Right after this, the prayer life of our Lord became constantly clear. In every moment in time that he got the opportunity, we read from the bible that he escaped to a solitary place just to pray, connect to the Father and commune with him.

Again the bible speaks to reveal certain instances of the Lord's life of prayer;

> Immediately he made the disciples get into
> The boat and go before him to the other side, while he
> Dismissed the crowds. And after he had dismissed the crowds,
> He went up on the mountain by himself to pray.
> When evening came, he was there alone,
> Matthew 14:23

> And it came to pass about eight days
> After these sayings, he took Peter and John and James,
> And went up into a mountain to pray. And as he prayed,
> The fashion of his countenance was altered, and
> His raiment was white and glistering.
> Luke 9:28

> When Jesus therefore perceived
> That they would come and take him by force,
> To make him a king, he departed again into
> A mountain himself alone.
> John 6:15

It is good to know and understand some of the ways in and through which the Lord conversed and communed with the Father to maintain their relationship. This is what I personally consider as a heaven-earth kind of relationship connecting heaven with the earth in and through prayer. Yes, it is like connecting God with man on earth in and through prayer. Our Father is in heaven but his presence is everywhere and though we are here on earth, he is still with us, in us and for us as well. The shortest way or means to get connected with our Father and him with us is by means of prayer. Prayer establishes us with God's divine covenant in and through his Son in whose name all prayers are answered. No wonder prayer seems to be the only thing the disciples openly and boldly asked the Lord to teach them.

> And it came to pass, that,
> As he was praying in a certain place, when he ceased,
> One of his disciples said unto him, Lord, teach us to pray,
> As John also taught his disciples.
> John 11:1

In many places in the bible, the Lord spoke and taught about prayer to us, some with reasons of why there is the need of prayer in the life of his followers.

> And he spake a parable unto them to this end,
> That men ought always to pray, and not to faint;
> Luke 18:1

I believe the Lord did teach them more than just prayer. I also believe he might have taught them the importance of the relationship that is involved with the God they are praying to; not just as a God but also as a Father. Father means source and giver of life. Not only the source and giver of life, but also the source upon which one can solely and totally depend for all and everything that concerns the life he gives as well. So he taught the disciples;

> But thou, when thou prayest,
> Enter into thy closet, and when thou hast shut thy door,
> Pray to thy Father which is in secret; and thy Father
> Which seeth in secret shall reward thee openly.
> Matthew 6:6
> (2 Kings. 4:33; Isaiah. 26:20)

In the Lord's teaching on prayer, he also taught us to watch alongside of prayer for the things that would come upon the world and all people in it. This was in order for us to escape from being taking into temptation by them. Again he said to the disciples and to us as well;

> For as a snare shall it come on all
> Them that dwell on the face of the whole earth
> Watch ye therefore, and pray always, that ye may be accounted
> Worthy to escape all these things that shall come to pass,
> And to stand before the Son of man
> Luke 21:35-36

And whatever the Lord spoke and said to the disciples then; is also meant for us now in these days. If he told them to watch as they prayed, not only for the will of God the Father to be done but to also know the will of God for their lives on earth; it is also meant for us to watch and pray for the same purpose. Again he told them why the need of a prayer life;

> Watch and pray,
> That ye enter not into temptation:
> The spirit indeed is willing, but the flesh is weak.
> Matthew 26:41

In another place of his teaching on prayer, the Lord reveals how through a prayer life, the enemy could be subdued under the believer's feet when he said and taught us this way;

> But I say unto you, Love your enemies,
> Bless them that curse you, do good to them that hate you,
> And pray for them which despitefully use you, and persecute you;
> That ye may be the children of your Father which is in heaven:
> For he maketh his sun to rise on the evil and on the good,
> And sendeth rain on the just and on the unjust
> Matthew 5:44-45
> (Luke 23:34; Acts 7:60; 2 Timothy 4:16; 1 Peter. 3:9)

But the apostle Paul by inspiration of the Holy Spirit gave clarity as to why praying for them that despitefully uses us when he preached to the church in Rome. He put it this way;

> Bless them which persecute you:
> Bless, and curse not.
> Romans 12:14

Then he went on further to assure us;

> Therefore if thine enemy hunger, feed him;
> If he thirsts, give him drink: for in so doing
> Thou shalt heap coals of fire
> On his head
> Romans 12:20

CHAPTER THREE

POSITION OF THE CROSS OF CHRIST

••••••••••••••••••••

THE CROSS OF JESUS Christ plays an important role in the life of every person on earth and in this world. It may not matter whether the person is born again or not. It does not as well matter in terms of geographical position. Everything that has to do with the cross in relations with the power that is in it affects and influences the life of every person in creation as far as Jehovah God is concerned.

However, there is something equally important to know as far as the position of the cross of Christ is concerned. And I am not talking about the physical position of the cross of Jesus Christ in between the two thieves, or on the hills of Golgotha; all of which are good in terms of their prophetic fulfillments. It is the spiritual position of the cross in relations to the sinner and the righteous or the believer and the unbeliever in the world that motivates me to want to share this revelation. We will be more concerned with the spiritual or the unseen position of the cross of Christ as far as the sinner or the unbeliever and the righteous or the unrighteous are concerned.

From the spiritual perspective, the cross of Christ stands in between God and the world. It stands between God and mankind. It stands between light and darkness. It stands between heaven and earth. It stands between the two kingdoms of God and Satan. It stands between good and evil. It stands between healing and sickness as well as diseases. It stands between liberty and captivity. It stands between freedom or deliverance and bondage. It stands between salvation or life and death. It stands in between blessing and curse. And in standing between all these and many more, the cross of Christ serves as an unseen bridge of division between two sides of life by which one can cross from one side to the other.

There are two positional sides to the cross of Jesus Christ which I refer to as the before and the after or beyond. On one side and a place of the cross are a people that are before the cross and there is another side and a place of the cross where some people are after or beyond the cross. People before the cross are yet to cross over by the cross. People beyond the cross have already crossed over to where they are by means of the cross. A person's position or place on the earth and in this world is either before or beyond the cross. There is no middle position where anybody is made to stay or abide at the cross. In fact, there is nowhere in the word of God to suggest that it is the intention of the Lord to keep any person at the cross. On the contrary, is the intention of the Lord God that people would be drawn to the cross of Christ; and by the cross of Christ, cross over and be transferred from one side of the cross unto the other side after or beyond the cross which is better and glorious.

This is all what most if not all of this book is about and draws attention to the reader, be it a believer or the non-believer. You see, one of the main purposes of this book is to bring awareness into the body of Christ or the church of Jesus Christ as to where everything that happened before, on and after the cross helps to shape up one's personal present position and identity for being in Christ with Christ also in him. Understanding this revelation will help many a people in the kingdom of God to know and define their God giving position in Christ and in life as well as their position of dominion, power and authority and how to appropriate it right here on earth. It will also help identify on which side a person belongs to in life and the power or the authority that connects him to whichever side a person might belong to. On some occasions in the bible, the Lord Jesus Christ used certain parables which many are not aware of the light it throws on the position of mankind in terms of the cross; and how it serves as a partition between the kingdom of God and that of Satan with their subsequent characteristics. One such parable includes the Wheat and Tares parable. In this parable the Lord taught us of how the wheat which is growing together with the tares would in the end be separated from one another at the time of harvest. This can be found and read in Matthew 13:24-30. Another parable of similarity to this revelation is the Goat and Sheep parable where the Lord taught us of how the sheep would also be separated from the goats during the final judgment. This can also be found and read in Matthew 25:31-34. So also it is in the unseen or the spiritual realm in connection with the cross of Christ and its present position. The cross of Christ serves to give an identity of a wheat, tares, goat or sheep in the unseen world. You see, the Lord Jesus Christ taught us of being in the world but not of it (John 17:14)

It is good to know that the present position of the cross in its spiritual sense is no more limited to Jerusalem. Neither is it limited to Golgotha or between the two thieves. The spiritual position of the cross of Christ goes beyond that and extends to the entire world and affects and influences the human race. What divides and separates the human race or people in the world are not the natural geographical boundaries of nations and countries. Neither is it their race, tribe or tongue. It is not even wars or the east and west ideologies and philosophies of government. Behind all these are forces, be it of light or darkness and of God or Satan. Don't forget that there are only two forces that seek to influence this world being that of God and Satan.

What actually divides people in the world is the cross of Calvary if we can understand the world to be of the two spiritual kingdoms of God and Satan; if we can understand the world to be of good and evil, and if we can understand the world to be of light and darkness with the battle for the soul of man raging on. This is where though the cross of Christ divides the human race; the people of God's kingdom of light and good being the wheat and the sheep are growing together alongside the people of Satan's kingdom of darkness and evil being the tares and the goats. This is what is going to bring about the separations of the human race in the last days of which the Lord shares in the two parables.

However the manifested separation would be seen in the last days where God says he will send his angels to harvest and gather together the wheat and burn the tares. This is how the bible records it;

> Let both grow together until the harvest:
> And in the time of harvest I will say to the reapers,
> Gather ye together first the tares, and bind them
> In bundles to burn them: but gather
> The wheat into my barn
> Matthew 13:30

Just as in a similar way, the sheep will be separated from the goats during the final judgment at the coming of the Son of Man; people will also be separated in the last days though we are all mixed up at least for now. In talking about the Son of Man coming in his glory at the final judgment during the harvest and separation, the bible says;

> And before him shall be gathered all nations:
> And he shall separate them one from another, as a shepherd
> Divideth his sheep from the goats: And he shall set the sheep
> On his right hand, but the goats on the left. Then shall the King
> Say unto them on his right hand, Come, ye blessed of my Father,
> Inherit the kingdom prepared for you from the foundation
> Of the world:
> Matthew 25:32-34

The phrase "and before him shall be gathered all nations," means that all nations are affected by the works of the cross of Calvary; directly or indirectly. With this in mind, we should be able to see the position of the cross of Christ with the spiritual eyes in order to understand its works in connection with people and nations of the world. It will also help us to know the people of the kingdom of God and the kingdom of Satan both of which are in this world. Another great thing that throws light on how all nations of the world might be affected directly or indirectly by the works of Christ on the cross is a scripture many of us may know. The scripture reads:

> For God so loved the world,
> That he gave his only begotten Son, that whosoever

Believeth in him should not perish, but have everlasting life.
For God sent not his Son into the world to condemn the world;
But that the world through him might be saved.
John 3:16-17

Here, the bible reveals that God's love for which made him send his only begotten Son was not for a few people but for the entire whole world of all nations, tribes and tongues. It should also be noted, Jesus Christ did not die for a few handful of people or some nations but that he died for the whole entire human race to bring salvation to the world. The bible says that Jesus Christ, Son of the living God who created and loved the world so much; died for the entire human race;

And they sung a new song, saying,
Thou art worthy to take the book, and to open
The seals thereof: for thou wast slain, and hast redeemed us
To God by thy blood out of every kindred, and
Tongue, and people, and nation;
Revelation 5:9

Through the works of the cross, the blood of Jesus Christ was shed to bring redemption to the world of every kindred, tongue, people and nation. It is therefore no wonder when in the parable of the sheep and goats, the bible says that "all nations shall be gathered before him" for separation and judgment. It shows how it does not seem to matter where a person may be living. Neither does it matter in terms of a person's race, colour or creed. No matter who a person might be or come from, Jesus Christ died and shed his precious blood through his works on the cross for the redemption of all mankind, from every nation, tribe, tongue and kindred. This is one of the many foundations for which the cross of Christ affects all nations, all people, all race, all tribes, all kindreds and all tongues. In one episode of the apostle John in the book of Revelation, he recalls of how people of all nations were seen standing before the throne of God;

> After this I beheld, and, lo, a great multitude,
> Which no man could number, of all nations, and kindreds,
> And people, and tongues, stood before the throne,
> And before the Lamb, clothed with white robes,
> And palms in their hands;
> Revelation 7:9

Again, knowing that he through the works of the cross and the shedding of his blood for the redemption of all mankind, God's salvation has become available for all mankind to receive; Jesus Christ commissioned his disciples to go into the entire world with the Gospel;

> And Jesus came and spake unto them,
> Saying, All power is given unto me in heaven and in earth.
> Go ye therefore, and teach all nations, baptizing them
> In the name of the Father, and of the Son,
> And of the Holy Ghost:
> Matthew 28:18-19

> And he said unto them,
> Go ye into all the world, and preach the gospel
> To every creature
> Mark 16:15

Then the apostle John in the book of Revelation also reveals;

> And I saw another angel fly in the midst of heaven,
> Having the everlasting gospel to preach unto them that dwell
> On the earth, and to every nation, and kindred, and tongue, and people,
> Saying with a loud voice, Fear God, and give glory to him;
> For the hour of his judgment is come: and worship him
> That made heaven, and earth, and the sea,
> And the fountains of waters
> Revelation 14:6-7

Now, just as Jesus Christ came into the world for all human races and just as he died and shed his precious blood on the cross to bring redemption to the world and all human races; so shall he come to judge the entire world of all nations, tribes, kindreds and tongues.

AT THE CROSS

At the cross, there were certain things that were brought to an end as far as their power and operations are concerned. They were made to be finished according to the will, plans and purposes of God through the works of Christ and the shedding of his blood on the cross. These are things which have been made ready for us to be able to live by. They are things which we can walk in by faith to appropriate them for our lives and in our lives right here on earth and in this world.

You see, God's divine encounter for mankind and with mankind is and would always be at the cross where his only begotten Son Jesus Christ was sacrificed for the salvation of mankind. It is only at the cross that any soul can have a true experience of repentance and forgiveness of sins. It is only at the cross that any soul can experience true salvation, deliverance and healing as well as peace in life.

Every single soul needs to have an encounter with the cross in order to be right with God. I believe that to be the only way for mankind to be restored back into divine relationship with God. It is the only open but narrow way of access into the kingdom of heaven (Matthew 7:13)

It is not only good to know but to also believe that every position, every power and every authority that the devil might have over the souls of men has been made to end up at the cross. So are the powers or works of the flesh and the curses of sin, death and poverty; they all have been made to end and cease their operations at the cross. You see, the moment a person is transferred and made to go beyond the cross, that person is redeemed by the works of the cross and the shed blood of Jesus Christ. The person becomes secured in Christ Jesus where the powers of the devil or of darkness have no more dominion over that person because of the things that took place at the cross.

And the things which took place at the cross have given us a divine security and authority in the kingdom of God though we might be here on earth. These are the very things we need to appropriate them as well right here on earth. These are not the things we need to wait and die before needing them. These things are for us to use right here on earth.

At the cross, Crucifixion of the body of Jesus Christ took place. After he was tried before Pilate and Pilate could not release him to go because of the crowd, the bible says that he gave Jesus Christ up to be crucified.

> Then released he Barabbas unto them:
> And when he had scourged Jesus, he
> Delivered him to be crucified
> Matthew 27:26

> And they crucified him,
> And parted his garments, casting lots:
> That it might be fulfilled which was spoken
> By the prophet, They parted my garments among them,
> And upon my vesture did they cast lots.
> Matthew 27:35

However unknown to the crowd and the Jewish leaders who agitated for Jesus Christ to be crucified, this was in the plans of God to bring redemption and salvation to mankind (1Corinthians 2:7-8)

This crucifixion of the body of Jesus Chris on the cross, led to the shedding of his blood on the cross. We should remember that the body of Jesus Christ by which he came through the virgin Mary and which was nailed to the cross was specially prepared for him by God (Hebrews 10:5). It was a body which was purposed to serve as a sacrificial lamb and whose blood will be used for God's covenant with all mankind (Matthew 26:26). It was the shedding of his blood on the cross that brought redemption to the whole human race...

> And they sung a new song, saying,
> Thou art worthy to take the book, and to open

The seals thereof: for thou wast slain, and hast redeemed
Us to God by thy blood out of every kindred,
And tongue, and people, and nation;
Revelation 5:9

The apostle Peter in his first letter adds something to throw light on how the blood of Jesus Christ brought about redemption to mankind when he said;

Forasmuch as ye know that ye
Were not redeemed with corruptible things,
As silver and gold, from your vain conversation received
By tradition from your fathers; But with the precious
Blood of Christ, as of a lamb without
Blemish and without spot:
1Peter 1:18

In whom we have
Redemption through his blood,
Even the forgiveness of sins:
Colossians 1:14

So therefore, by the crucifixion and the shedding of his blood, the death of Jesus Christ, Son of the living God took place not only for a few people, but for all mankind.

Through his death on the cross, Jesus Christ took all the weaknesses, all the infirmities, all the diseases and all the sicknesses of all mankind in his body and nailed them all onto the cross. The apostle Peter by inspiration of the Holy Ghost put it this way;

Who his own self bare our sins in his own body
On the tree, that we, being dead to sins, Should live
Unto righteousness: by whose stripes ye were healed.
1Peter 2:24
(Isaiah 53:4; Matthew 8:17; Hebrews 9:28)

At the cross and through the cross, divine transformation and transfiguration of mankind took place by a divine translation into a new kingdom where we obtained a new nature and a new identity in Christ. The apostle Paul in his letter to the Colossian church talked about this translation where he revealed it this way;

> Who hath delivered us from
> The power of darkness, and hath translated us
> Into the kingdom of his dear Son:
> Colossians 1:13

In the kingdom of his dear Son, there is where we find ourselves as new creations with all the old things passed away and everything having become a new (2Corinthians 5:17).

I call it a miracle of salvation, deliverance and healing. In fact, a newness of life was born out of the cross and a total divine exchange of life took place at the cross where Jesus Christ became who and what mankind were and supposed to be, for mankind to become who and what he is. The bible reveals it this way;

> For he hath made him to be sin for us,
> Who knew no sin; that we might be made
> The righteousness of God in him
> 2Corinthians 5:21

At the cross and through the cross, an eternal defeat but also an eternal victory took place over the arch enemy Satan. Satan, with all his power was eternally defeated and victory over him was eternally won by Christ for God's people. Every power and authority Satan may have to exercise it over mankind ended at the cross. Beyond the cross with the resurrected and glorified Christ, Satan cannot operate to prevail. And I believe it is based upon this foundation beyond the cross where Satan cannot operate to prevail that our lord Jesus Christ declared the building his church. He said and assured us;

> And I say also unto thee,
> That thou art Peter, and upon this rock
> I will build my church; and the gates of hell
> Shall not prevail against it
> Matthew 16:18

So our Lord Jesus Christ declared;

> And Jesus came and spake unto them, saying,
> All power is given unto me in heaven and in earth.
> Matthew 28:18

And from the all power and authority given unto him; our lord Jesus Christ has also empowered his Church. So that if the church of Jesus Christ will rise to live and walk by this power, Satan cannot in any way prevail against his church. This is how he reveals it;

> And he said unto them,
> I beheld Satan as lightning fall from heaven.
> Behold, I give unto you power to tread on serpents
> And scorpions, and over all the power of the enemy:
> And nothing shall by any means hurt you.
> Luke 10:18-19
> (Philippians 2:8-11)

The flesh and its works and lusts were overcome and defeated at the cross (Romans 8:8-9); so also was the world with all its lusts defeated (John 16:33). All these divine victories and possibly many more others that took place at the cross, combines to usher us into the realms of God's planned and purposed glory for us in and through Christ as a new breed of God's people.

Again, all these unseen miracles that took place at the cross gave birth to all and everything that can be enjoyed beyond the cross; and all and everything that are beyond the cross are located in the glorified Chrit at the Father's right hand side.

THE KINGDOM OF GOD

The kingdom of God is real and in this world but spiritual and everlasting. It is a kingdom of eternal life and reigns above all other form of kingdoms (Daniel 2:44). It is the realm of God's reign and governance based on the rule of his word and principles of righteousness. The bible says that the scepter of God's kingdom is a scepter of righteousness (Hebrews 1:8). In other words you cannot find the kingdom of God in operation without his righteousness prevailing (Matthew 6:33). It can be in a person or in a place, that is wherever the word of God is being exercised and being adhered to; God's kingdom is at work.

At the coming of Jesus Christ into this world, came also the kingdom of God upon the earth, but after the works of the cross and the shed blood of Jesus Christ, the kingdom of God became spiritually established (Acts 1:2-3). God's kingdom on earth can now be seen, entered in and be inherited. Though the violent should take it by force (Matthew 11:12), the works of the cross and the shed blood of Jesus Christ have opened the divine door which makes it possible for all mankind to be able to see, enter in and inherit it by faith in Christ. (John 3:3-5). The truth is that, there is more to the kingdom of God than just what is talked about on this page and much can be learnt and known from the great book itself which we call the Bible.

However, the physical manifestation and establishment of God's kingdom on earth and in this world will be when the Son of God, Jesus Christ will return again (Acts 1:9-11; Luke 21:27). Through the open door by faith in Christ Jesus, God has made a people unto himself spiritually (Colossians 1:13-14; 1Peter 2:9). These are the people of the kingdom of God in this world who live to manifest and demonstrate the power and the glory in and through their lives (Matthew 5:14-16). The people of God's kingdom are them that have received, believed and have accepted Jesus Christ as their personal Lord and Savior. They are a people that have been redeemed and purchased by the precious blood of Jesus Christ. They are a people that have been delivered from the power of darkness and translated by God through the cross into the kingdom of his beloved Son. They are a people that are in this world but not of this world and whose kingdom is also not of this world. The Lord Jesus Christ revealed it unto us in his prayer to the Father before he ascended into heaven when he said;

> I have given them thy word;
> And the world hath hated them, because
> They are not of the world, even as I am not of the world.
> John 17:14

And because they are not of this world and depend not on this world for anything; they also do not get conformed to this world (Romans 12:2). They are a people that are in the flesh but not of the flesh (2Corinthians 10:3; Romans 8:8). They are dead with Christ and respond no more to the things of the flesh in Christ. This is how the word of God which is the bible reveals it;

> Wherefore if ye be dead with Christ
> From the rudiments of the world, why, as though
> Living in the world, are ye subject to ordinances,
> Colossians 2:20
> (Romans 6:3; Colossians 3:1,3)

These are in Christ with Christ in them as new creations (2Corinthians 5:17). Their lives are spiritually fused together in love, unity and harmony where Christ is increased and formed in their lives (1Corinthians 6:17; Ephesians 4:19). They are them that have the spirit and the life of Christ in them (Romans 8:9). They live in the spirit and walk in the spirit (Galatians 5:25) with no condemnation upon their lives because they have become the righteousness of God in Christ (Romans 8:1-3; 2Corinthians 5:20). The Holy Spirit is their teacher, leader and guide into the truth of all things that pertains to their eternal life in this world.

IDENTIFYING WITH THE CROSS

> Giving thanks unto the Father,
> Which hath made us meet to be partakers
> Of the inheritance of the saints in light: Who hath delivered us
> From the power of darkness, and hath translated us
> Into the kingdom of his dear Son:
> Colossians 1:12-13

Life in Christ is identifying with the cross. A person cannot have life and be in Christ without having had a divine encounter with Christ at the cross. In other words, one has to go through the cross in order to have life in Christ. Many may not have realized it but the moment we were lifting up our hands to confess Jesus Christ as our personal Lord and Saviour; we were also having a personal encounter with him at the cross. We were shedding off our old sinful and garbage nature and leaving them at the cross. We were positioning ourselves for the miracle of spiritual death and a divine translation to the other side beyond the cross. We were identifying ourselves with what took place in terms of Christ's death, burial and resurrection in relation with our lives becoming a new in him. Or simply put, becoming a born again new creation in him.

The bible says that we died with him on the cross, were buried and also raised with him which actually ushered us together with him into where he now is after the resurrection. The apostle Paul in his letter to the Roman Church revealed it this way;

> Therefore we are buried with him
> By baptism into death: that like as Christ was raised up
> From the dead by the glory of the Father, even so we also
> Should walk in newness of life. For if we have been
> Planted together in the likeness of his death,
> We shall be also in the likeness of his
> Resurrection
> Romans 6:4-5

So therefore, we identify ourselves with the cross of Christ in connection with the new life which we have received in Christ; a life that came about because of Christ and his works on the cross. You see, for the Believer or him that is born again and therefore has Christ in his life, the Cross of Christ is no more before him. The cross is now behind him having attained that miracle of spiritual translation. He has crossed over to beyond the cross so that when he turns to look back, the cross of Christ is what he or she sees between him and the old past world from where he was before. If we can see it from this perspective, that is with our spiritual eye; we can also understand that, to go back again into the old past sinful nature of the world would mean going through the cross once again (Hebrews 6:4-6). A divine translation has taken place as the bible declares in Colossians 1:13.

While the cross becomes a place and position of the past; it also becomes the source out of where the new life is born through the resurrection of our Lord Jesus Christ (1Peter 1:3). What is ahead of the believer in Christ is the eternal newness of life in the abundance of God's grace, God's righteousness and god's glory ready to be explored together with the Holy Spirit. He has entered into the realm of God's abundant grace, righteousness and the glory of God which is in Christ Jesus. The apostle Peter in his first letter to the churches in Diaspora assured them with the following scripture;

> Blessed be the God and Father
> Of our Lord Jesus Christ, which according to his
> Abundant mercy hath begotten us again unto a lively hope
> By the resurrection of Jesus Christ from the dead,
> To an inheritance incorruptible, and undefiled, and that
> Fadeth not away, reserved in heaven for you,
> 1Peter 1:3-4

IDENTITY BEFORE THE CROSS

> Wherefore, as by one man
> Sin entered into the world and death by sin;

> And so death passed upon all men,
> For that all have sinned:
> Romans 5:12

Our identity before the cross is that of an unbelieving sinner. An unbelieving sinner still has no relations with God. As far as the unbelieving sinner or person who is not yet born again and therefore has no relationship with God in and through Christ is concerned, the cross of Christ is always standing before him. And the cross of Jesus Christ stands as the loving open arms of God ever to receive and welcome the sinner to cross over to yonder. Such a person is still a sinner before the eyes of God. He needs to be redeemed unto repentance and forgiveness of sins in order to be saved in and through the works of the cross and the shed blood of Jesus Christ. The bible puts it this way in declaring our identity before the cross;

> For all have sinned,
> And come short of the glory of God
> Romans 3:23

Our identity before the cross is that of one fallen short of the glory of God. Not only are we fallen short of the glory of God; we also fall short of his grace and his righteousness all because of sin. The sinner is not a sinner because of what he does wrong or wickedly. The sinner is a sinner because of the sin gene inherited through sin and the subsequent fall of Adam and Eve in the Garden of Eden when they disobeyed and choose their own will instead of God's will. This was after Satan through the serpent in the Garden of Eden, had tempted Eve by causing her to disobey God's command of not eating from the forbidden fruit. The story can be read in Genesis Chapter three.

Through this disobedience of Adam, his sin and fall; the whole mankind lost all relations with God his creator. Man died spiritually though which manifested in the physical death as well. Death simply means separation from God. This loss of connection or separation from a relationship with God allowed sin to enter into the world with its curses of poverty, sickness, diseases and death, both spiritual and physical. This is how the bible says it in speaking about Adam;

> For as by one man's disobedience
> Many were made sinners, so by the obedience
> Of one (Christ) shall many be made righteous
> Romans 5:19

The unbeliever as a sinner, still lives under the bondage of sin and Satan has a grip on him or her. He lives in Satan's kingdom of darkness and needs to be delivered by the power of God through the cross. However, such a person needs to believe and receive Christ into his life as a personal Lord and Saviour. This is the only way such a person can be redeemed and be saved by the works of the cross and the shed blood of Jesus Christ. The bible says;

> That if thou shalt confess with thy mouth
> The Lord Jesus, and shalt believe in thine heart
> That God hath raised him from the dead,
> Thou shalt be saved.
> Romans 10:9

This would subsequently deliver and lead them out of darkness into God's marvelous light (1Peter 2:9). The apostle Paul in one of his letters to the Corinthian Church said something which helps throw some light on this matter. He said;

> But if our gospel be hid, it is hid to them that are lost:
> In whom the god of this world hath blinded the minds
> Of them which believe not, lest the light of
> The glorious gospel of Christ,
> Who is the image of God
> Should shine unto them
> 2Corinthians 4:3-4

The unbelieving sinner cannot believe because as the bible reveals, their hearts are blinded to the hearing of the gospel of Jesus Christ which in itself is the power of God to save them. What the apostle Paul wrote to the church in Rome can help throw some light on this point. He said;

> For I am not ashamed of the gospel of Christ:
> For it is the power of God unto salvation
> To everyone that believeth;
> To the Jew first, and also to the Greek
> Romans 1:16

This can confirm that it takes the supernatural working miracle of preaching the true gospel of Jesus Christ to save the sinner. It is by the preaching of the gospel of Jesus Christ that God calls men through Jesus Christ unto himself. Jesus Christ is the straight and narrow way through which mankind can get to God. Coming to Jesus Christ is coming to God. And coming to God cannot be possible except by Jesus Christ, which is only through the cross. So therefore, all is not lost for the unbelieving sinner who is taken in bondage of darkness by Satan. Jesus Christ, Saviour of the lost world and Son of the living God, Jehovah the Great I am, offers the only hope of the glory, the grace and the righteousness which mankind lost through sin. This is how the apostle Paul speaks of it;

> To whom God would make known
> What is the riches of the glory of this mystery
> Among the Gentiles; which is Christ in you
> The hope of glory:
> Colossians 1:27

These are some few of the many scriptures that the Lord Jesus Christ used to throw some light on himself as the source of connection to the Father and Saviour of the lost world. Jesus said;

> Jesus answered,
> Verily, verily, I say unto thee,
> Except a man be born of water and of the Spirit,

He cannot enter into the kingdom of God.
John 3:5

No man can come to me,
Except the Father which hath sent me draw him:
And I will raise him up at the last day.
John 6:44

Enter ye in at the strait gate:
For wide is the gate, and broad is the way,
That leadeth to destruction, and many there be
Which go in there at: Because strait is the gate,
And narrow is the way, which leadeth unto life,
And few there be that find it.
Matthew 7:13-14

Jesus saith unto him,
I am the way, the truth, and the life:
No man cometh unto the Father, but by me.
John 14:6

I am the door:
By me if any man enter in, he shall be saved,
And shall go in and out, and find pasture.
John 10:9

So therefore, whoever and whatever is before the cross is also outside of Christ. It means that whoever and whatever is outside of Christ abides in darkness. And whoever and whatever is before the cross and outside of Christ, abiding in darkness; also abides in sin and is controlled by Satan (2Corinthians 4:4). You see, in regards to the operations of all these things combined, every person and for that matter everything that is before the cross, gets their identity or is identified based on their position before the cross. But the one in Christ has his or her new creation identity in Christ (2Corinthians 5:17), who is no more on the cross but in his glorified position beyond the cross. The believer is therefore identified as a new creation not with Christ before or on the cross but with the resurrected and glorified Christ beyond the cross.

CHAPTER FOUR

NO MORE ON THE CROSS

• •

WE SHOULD LEARN TO know and understand that the activities or the works which were in the will of the Father for our Lord Jesus Christ before he went to the cross is forever finished. All its benefits of blessings and inheritance are also fully established for the believer. Not only that, but his activities or works that were in the Father's will for him on the cross itself has also been finished to fully establish God's plan of salvation for all mankind. So therefore, we no longer have to look for another works of Christ before the cross; neither do we have to expect another physical crucifixion of our Lord on the cross again. We should rather look beyond the cross in order to see and identify with the results of the finished work of our Lord Jesus Christ, both before and on the cross. Beyond the cross are the culminated results of all that we can identify ourselves with as far as the life, death, burial and resurrection of our Lord Jesus Christ is concerned.

The Lord Jesus Christ went from the cross to the grave. His crucified body was taken down from off the cross to be buried in the grave. So the body of the Lord Jesus Christ was not made to remain hanging on the cross. His body was taken from the cross. He was buried. He was laid in the tomb of a man called Joseph who was from the town of Arimathaea. The bible records it this way;

> Joseph of Arimathaea,
> An honourable counsellor, which also waited
> For the kingdom of God, came, and went in boldly
> Unto Pilate, and craved the body of Jesus.

> And Pilate marvelled if he were already dead:
> And calling unto him the centurion, he asked him
> Whether he had been any while dead. And when
> He knew it of the centurion; he gave the body to Joseph.
> And he bought fine linen, and took him down,
> And wrapped him in the linen, and laid him in a sepulchre
> Which was hewn out of a rock, and rolled a stone
> Unto the door of the sepulchre
> Mark 15:43-46

The significance of knowing that the body of the Lord Jesus Christ was buried is enormous. It fulfills prophecy and plays important role in God's plan of salvation, deliverance and victory for mankind. Christ's victory needed to be fully established as Lord of lords and King of kings over all the powers that be, not only in the heavens and on the earth, but also over all the powers of darkness under the earth! Though this victory was already won in the realm of glory as we read in the book of Revelation chapter 5; this victory needed to be manifested and be fulfilled in the natural realm. Hence, his coming to be flesh to dwell among men as the apostle John reveals;

> And the Word was made flesh,
> And dwelt among us, (and we beheld his glory,
> The glory as of the only begotten of the Father,)
> Full of grace and truth
> John 1:14
> (Philippians 2:8-11; Ephesians 1:9-10)

Buried in the grave, the victory of the works of Christ before and on the cross continued to prevail. There in the grave, Christ entered into the satanic arena of darkness to completely finish his work of salvation and deliverance of mankind from the powers of darkness. I can only imagine how dark the satanic arena of bondage and captivity could be without any light. But I can also believe how on that day, the glorious presence and light of our Lord and Saviour Jesus Christ appeared to shine in that satanic dungeon to subdue, overpower and conquer all power of darkness. I believe it to be what the bible records in the book of John as this;

> In him was life;
> And the life was the light of men.
> And the light shineth in darkness;
> And the darkness comprehended it not.
> John 1:4-5

Not only did the light of Christ's presence subdued to overpower and conquer Satan and his kingdom of darkness but the whole kingdom of Satan was defeated, spoiled and taken captive. The captivity has now become captive as the bible records;

> Wherefore he saith, when he ascended up on high,
> He led captivity captive, and gave gifts unto men.
> (Now that he ascended, what is it but that he also
> Descended first into the lower parts of the earth?
> He that descended is the same also
> That ascended up far above all heavens,
> That he might fill all things.)
> Ephesians 4:8-10

> And having spoiled principalities and powers,
> He made a shew of them openly,
> Triumphing over them in it
> Colossians 2:15

> 19 And what is the exceeding greatness
> Of his power to us- ward who believe, according to
> The working of his mighty power, which he wrought
> In Christ, when he raised him from the dead, and set him
> At his own right hand in the heavenly places, far above
> All principality, and power, and might, and dominion,

> And every name that is named, not only in this world,
> But also in that which is to come:
> Ephesians 1:19-21

> That at the name of Jesus
> Every knee should bow, of things in heaven,
> And things in earth, and things under the earth;
> And that every tongue should confess
> That Jesus Christ is Lord, to the
> Glory of God the Father
> Philippians 2:10-11

Christ overcame him that had the keys of death, grave and hell. There in the dungeons of satanic darkness, the triumphant Lord of lords and King of kings snatched from him who through death, grave and hell had taken captive of mankind; the keys of hell and death. Satan therefore has no more power to take captive of mankind anymore. The Lord Jesus Christ through his death, burial and resurrection has fully and completely disarmed him of all his power (Matthew 28:18; Luke 10:19; Matthew 10:1). In his appearance unto the apostle John on the island of Patmos, we hear the Lord Jesus Christ confirming this with his words to the apostle;

> I am he that liveth, and was dead;
> And, behold, I am alive for evermore, Amen;
> And have the keys of hell and of death.
> Revelation 1:18

Not only does the Lord has the keys of hell and death; he also has and possesses the keys of David;

> And to the angel of the church in
> Philadelphia write; these things saith he
> That is holy, he that is true,
> He that hath the key of David,
> He that openeth, and no man shutteth;

And shutteth, and no man openeth;
Revelation 3:7

The bible which is the word of God says; Jesus Christ was raised from the dead by the power of God. Oh Hallelujah! Death could not hold him in bondage; neither could the grave keep him. He resurrected.

NEITHER IS HE ANYMORE IN THE TOMB...

And as they were afraid,
And bowed down their faces to the earth,
They said unto them, why seek ye the living among
The dead? He is not here, but is risen: remember how
He spake unto you when he was yet in Galilee,
Luke 24:5-6

HE IS RISEN FROM THE DEAD AND ASCENDED INTO HEAVEN...

And when he had spoken these things,
While they beheld, he was taken up; and a cloud
Received him out of their sight. And while they looked
Steadfastly toward heaven as he went up, behold, two men stood
By them in white apparel; Which also said, Ye men of Galilee,
Why stand ye gazing up into heaven? this same Jesus,
Which is taken up from you into heaven
Shall so come in like manner as ye have
Seen him go into heaven
Acts 1:9-11

So then after the Lord had spoken unto them,
He was received up into heaven, and sat
On the right hand of God.
Mark 16:19

For Christ is not entered into the holy places
Made with hands, which are the figures of the true;
But into heaven itself, now to appear in
The presence of God for us:
Hebrews 9:24

Who is he that condemneth?
It is Christ that died, yea rather, that is risen again,
Who is even at the right hand of God,
Who also maketh intercession for us.
Romans 8:34

Wherefore he is able also to save them
To the uttermost that come unto God by him,
Seeing he ever liveth to make intercession for them.
Hebrews 7:25

AND ALIVE FOREVER MORE...

I am he that liveth, and was dead;
And, behold, I am alive for evermore, Amen;
And have the keys of hell and of death.
Revelation 1:18

And unto the angel of
The church in Smyrna write; These things
Saith the first and the last,
Which was dead, and is alive;
Revelation 2:8

No more on the cross and no more in the tomb but risen and ascended into the heavens, the Lord Jesus Christ has entered into his glory from where he came.

Then he said unto them,
O fools, and slow of heart to believe all
That the prophets have spoken: Ought not Christ
To have suffered these things, and to enter into his glory?
Luke 24:25-26
(Hebrews 12:2)

OUR GREAT HIGH PRIEST . . .

Wherefore, holy brethren,
Partakers of the heavenly calling,
Consider the Apostle and High Priest of
Our profession, Christ Jesus;
Hebrews 5:1

Seeing then that we have a great high priest,
That is passed into the heavens, Jesus the Son of God,
Let us hold fast our profession.
Hebrews 4:14

For consider him that endured
Such contradiction of sinners against himself,
Lest ye be wearied and faint in your minds
Hebrews 12:3

Wherefore in all things it behoved him
To be made like unto his brethren, that he might be
A merciful and faithful high priest in things
Pertaining to God, to make reconciliation
For the sins of the people
Hebrews 2:17
(Hebrews 5:1-2)

And having an high priest over
The house of God; Let us draw near
With a true heart in full assurance of faith,
Having our hearts sprinkled from an evil conscience,
And our bodies washed with pure water
Hebrews 10:21-22

For we have not an high priest
Which cannot be touched with the feeling
Of our infirmities; but was in all points tempted
Like as we are, yet without sin. Let us therefore
Come boldly unto the throne of grace, that we
May obtain mercy, and find grace
To help in time of need.
Hebrews 4:15-16

And God is able to make
All grace abound toward you;
That ye, always having all sufficiency
In all things, may abound to every good work:
2Corinthians 9:8
(Ephesians 2:10; 1Corinthians 1:4; 1Corinthians
15:10; 2Corinthians 13:14)

OUR GREAT INTERCESSOR . . .

For Christ is not entered into
The holy places made with hands, which are
The figures of the true; but into heaven itself,
Now to appear in the presence of God for us:
Hebrews 9:24

Who is he that condemneth?
It is Christ that died, yea rather, that is risen again,
Who is even at the right hand of God,

Who also maketh intercession for us.
Romans 8:34

But this man,
Because he continueth ever,
Hath an unchangeable priesthood.
Wherefore he is able also to save them
To the uttermost that come unto God by him,
Seeing he ever liveth to make intercession for them
Hebrews 7:24-25

All that the Father giveth me shall
Come to me; and him that cometh to me
I will in no wise cast out.
Matthew 6:37

THE SHEPHERD AND BISHOP OF OUR SOULS . . .

For ye were as sheep going astray;
But are now returned unto the Shepherd
And Bishop of your souls
1Peter 2:25

He shall feed his flock like a shepherd:
He shall gather the lambs with his arm,
And carry them in his bosom, and shall
Gently lead those that are with young
Isaiah 40:11

I am the good shepherd:
The good shepherd giveth his life
For the sheep
John 10:11

As the Father knoweth me,
Even so know I the Father: and I lay
Down My life for the sheep
John 10:15
(John 10:17-18; John 15:13; 1John 3:16; Matthew 20:28; mark 10:45)

Now the God of peace,
That brought again from the dead
Our Lord Jesus, that great shepherd of the sheep,
Through the blood of the everlasting covenant,
Make you perfect in every good work to do his will,
Working in you that which is well pleasing in his sight,
Through Jesus Christ; to whom be glory
Forever and ever. Amen.
Hebrews 13:20-21

OUR SOON COMING KING…

Which also said, ye men of Galilee,
Why stand ye gazing up into heaven? This same
Jesus, which is taken up from you into heaven,
Shall so come in like manner as ye have
Seen him go into heaven
Acts 1:11

And as he sat upon the Mount of Olives,
The disciples came unto him privately, saying,
Tell us, when shall these things be? And what shall
Be the sign of thy coming, and of the end of the world?
Matthew 24:3

For as the lightning cometh out of the east,
And shineth even unto the west; so shall also
The coming of the Son of man be
Matthew 24:27

And then shall appear the sign of
The Son of man in heaven: and then shall all
The tribes of the earth mourn, and they shall see
The Son of man coming in the clouds of heaven
With power and great glory
Matthew 24:30

And, behold, I come quickly;
And my reward is with me, to give every man
According as his work shall be. I am Alpha and Omega,
The beginning and the end, the first and the last
Revelation 22:12-13

NO ONE KNOWS WHEN…

And as he sat upon the Mount of Olives,
The disciples came unto him privately, saying,
Tell us, when shall these things be? And what shall be
The sign of thy coming, and of the end of the world?
And Jesus answered and said unto them,
Take heed that no man deceive you.
Matthew 24:3-4

But of that day and hour knoweth no man,
No, not the angels of heaven,
But my Father only
Matthew 24:36
(Acts 1:6-7; Daniel 2:21; Matthew 24:37-45)

But the day of the Lord will come
As a thief in the night; in the which the heavens
Shall pass away with a great noise, and the elements
Shall melt with fervent heat, the earth also and
The works that are therein shall be burned up.
2 Peter 3:10 (1Thessalonians 5:1-2)

Be ye also patient; stablish your hearts:
For the coming of the Lord draweth nigh.
James 5:8
(Luke 21:19; Matthew 24:12-13)

BUT HOW READY ARE YOU…

Therefore be ye also ready:
For in such an hour as ye think not
The Son of man cometh
Matthew 24:43

Watch therefore: for ye Know not
What hour your Lord doth come.
Matthew 24:42

Take ye heed,
Watch and pray: for ye know not
When the time is
Mark 13:33

CHAPTER FIVE

LOOKING UNTO JESUS

• •

> Looking unto Jesus
> The author and finisher of our faith;
> Who for the joy that was set before him endured
> The cross, despising the shame, and is set down at
> The right hand of the throne of God
> Hebrews 12:2

CHRIST JESUS AFTER THE cross is not the same Christ Jesus before he went to the cross in the flesh. Neither is he the same as the Christ Jesus that hanged on the cross with the body that born all the sins, sicknesses, diseases and infirmities of mankind. Much more, he is now the resurrected and glorified Christ Jesus with the name that is above every other name in heaven, on earth and under the earth; the name at the mention of which every knee bows and every tongue confesses that he is Lord to the glory of the Father (Philippians 2:8-11). And he is coming again, but coming as a different Christ than he first came as a child born of the Virgin Mary and as the Word that became flesh and dwelt among men. He shall come in glory and power to reign and to rule; and all eyes shall see him.

By his life before the cross, his suffering on the cross and after the cross through his resurrection and ascension into his present glorious position on the Father's right hand side; God the Father in heaven has completed and perfected all things that pertains unto eternal life for mankind. Now, the Father has through the Lord Jesus Christ in his present glorious position opened and made a way for mankind back into his glory for us which were lost through Adam in the Garden of Eden (Genesis 3). The bible says that living by eternal life in Christ Jesus has to do with knowing God and Jesus Christ as the Son of God on personal basis (John 17:3; 2Peter 1:2-3).

However, knowing him is not only limited to Christ Jesus as he was before the cross and on the cross, but more importantly as he is at present after his resurrection and ascension beyond the cross. This is good to know so that as we look up unto Jesus Christ to consider him as the author, finisher and perfecter of our faith and salvation, we will not look to him with our physical eyes but with our spiritual eyes which goes beyond as he was in the flesh before and on the cross. There is a scripture which I am so passionate about in the Apostle Paul's second letter to the Corinthian church. This scripture has really blessed me in knowing, understanding and believing in Christ Jesus in his present personality as the true Son of the living God. It throws some light on how we can look unto Christ through the spiritual eye of God's word. He said to the Corinthians, which I believe is also relevant to the church today;

> Wherefore henceforth
> Know we no man after the flesh:
> Yea, though we have known Christ
> After the flesh, yet now henceforth
> Know we him no more.
> 2Corinthians 5:16

By our spiritual eyes we see Christ Jesus beyond the cross as him who was dead but now lives and is alive forever more. We also can understand and see him as he was, is and is to come through how he revealed to the apostle John on the island of Patmos. The apostle John describes it as this;

> And when I saw him, I fell at his feet as dead.
> And he laid his right hand upon me, saying unto me,

> Fear not; I am the first and the last: I am he that liveth,
> And was dead; and, behold, I am alive for evermore,
> Amen; And have the keys of hell and of death.
> Revelation 1:17-18

He lives forevermore in eternity. So we can see that the resurrection power is beyond the cross (Ephesians 1:18-19). It is there beyond the cross that we see Christ Jesus as raised from the dead having overcome death, the grave and hell through the cross because none of them could hold him captive...

> Knowing that Christ being raised
> From the dead dieth no more; death hath
> No more dominion over him.
> Romans 6:9-10

The apostle Peter in his sermon after the outpouring of the Holy Spirit also declares the triumphant resurrection power of our Lord Jesus Christ over death. He says;

> Whom God hath raised up,
> Having loosed the pains of death: because
> It was not possible that he should be holden of it.
> Acts 2:24

> For to this end Christ both died,
> And rose, and revived, that he might be
> Lord both of the dead and living.
> Romans 14:9

It is beyond the cross that we see Christ Jesus as the victorious and triumphant conqueror over the devil (Hebrews 2:14), over sin (1John 3:5), over the flesh (1Peter 3:18) over the world (John 16:33); and over all powers that be (Matthew 28:18) . . .

> And having spoiled principalities
> And powers, he made a shew of them openly,
> Triumphing over them in it
> Colossians 2:15

WHERE I AM . . .

> In my Father's house are many mansions:
> if it were not so, I would have told you.
> I go to prepare a place for you.
> And if I go and prepare a place for you,
> I will come again, and receive you unto myself;
> That where I am, there ye may be also
> John 14:2-3

Having understood Jesus Christ in his present glorified position, there is one more important thing to know. This is the Lord's desire, plan and purpose for his followers to be where he is. If it is The Lord's desire for us to be where he is, then I believe also that the desire of his people, his body and his church should be for where he is. The Lord taught us;

> If any man serve me,
> Let him follow me; and where I am,
> There shall also my servant be
> If any man serves me, him will my
> Father honour
> John 12:26

Based on what the Lord has taught us; we should not look up unto him again as he was in the flesh before the cross or on the cross but as the one who after he has endured suffering on the cross, has entered into his glory and majesty (Luke 24:25-26).

Jesus Christ should be looked up unto at where he actually is; and as the risen Lord in his glory on the Father's right hand side

(Romans 8:34). He should be looked up unto as who he really is in connection with his present position and all what these have to do with his relationship with us who are born again and confesses our faith in him. In other words, do you see yourself as a born again new creation in him? Do you see yourself where he is in the heavenly places? (Ephesians 2:6)

The bible says that Christ Jesus has entered into the heavens for us, meaning that his presence there should also be seen or looked at in relation with us as well. He has gone there for us and through the eyes of faith; we should see him as being there for us. Not only that; we should be able to see ourselves there with him to fulfill his promise by faith. This is what the bible says about his entrance into heaven;

> For Christ is not entered into
> The holy places made with hands,
> Which are the figures of the true; but
> Into heaven itself, now to appear in
> The presence of God for us:
> Hebrews 9:24

And as we look up unto Jesus Christ in relation to ourselves, we can also understand the very heart beat of the Lord in how much he desires for us to be drawn closer to be where he is and wants to share all that he has accomplished in and through the cross with us as well. That is his glory. It is so amazing that all what Jesus Christ came to live suffer and died for was for us. Christ Jesus was not glorified before the cross; neither was Christ glorified on the cross. Christ Jesus was glorified after his suffering works on the cross and his resurrection from the dead (John 7:38-39; Luke 24:26; 1Peter 1:21; Philippians 2:8-11).

The word of God reveals that it is the will of the Father that Christ Jesus shared all his glory with us who have believed in him. So therefore, as we believe in him and look up unto him as our Lord and Saviour; we should also raise our faith to believe in the sharing of all that he has with him. Some of these include his life, death, burial, resurrection, and his position of power, glory and anointing, hallelujah!

> And all mine are thine,
> And thine are mine; and I am glorified in them.
> John 17:10

Christ Jesus in all his glory is actually glorified in us as his Body and Church according to the word of God. It is to say that his glory as shared with us can also be manifested, demonstrated and seen through them that have believed in him; and them in whom he abides (John 14:23). Once he abides in us, he can also manifest to show forth his glory and himself in and through us.

Indeed, he assured us in his prayer to the Father in the book of John concerning this desire of sharing his glory with us;

> And the glory which thou
> Gavest me I have given them;
> That they may be one, even as we are one:
> John 17:22

This is the glory the bible says the whole creation awaits for its manifestation in the true sons of God (Isaiah 60:1-2; Romans 8:17-19). And then again as a request unto the Father on our behalf, our Lord Jesus Christ asks the Father for us to be where he is in order to behold this glory, he said;

> Father, I will that they also,
> Whom thou hast given me, be with me
> Where I am; that they may behold my glory,
> Which thou hast given me: for thou lovedst me
> Before the foundation of the world
> John 17:24

I believe that the moment we believe, accept and come to be born again in Christ as new creations; we also come to the place where Christ is. A divine translation takes place from the old into a newness of life. This new birth also positions us to sharing all that Jesus Christ has including the Father's glory. One truth is that, his suffering did not bring him alone into his glory (Luke 24:25-26); his suffering also brought many sons, his Body and Church into the Father's glory where he is (Hebrews 2:9-11). The truth is that Father God has called us into his kingdom and glory in and through our Lord and Saviour Jesus Christ (1Peter 5:10; 1Thessalonians 2:12; Isaiah 60:1-2)

As we already know that Christ Jesus is glorified and sanctified in us and us in him, we as his Body should also learn how to live a sanctified and glorified life for him to manifest in and through us by the power of the Holy Spirit inside of us (Romans 8:14-16; 2Corinthians 3:17-18). And the bible which is the word of God talks of how the glory of Christ can be shared with us as heirs of God and joint-heirs with Christ;

> And if children, then heirs;
> Heirs of God and joint- heirs with Christ;
> If so be that we suffer with him, that we may
> Be also glorified together.
> Romans 8:17

In order to be where Christ Jesus is and to share in all that he has, the bible reveals that God the Father has raised us up to be seated with him in his present position on the Father's right hand side. This is for us to be where he is; something which every believer in Christ Jesus must grasp. This is how God's word puts it;

> And hath raised us up together,
> And made us sit together in heavenly
> Places in Christ Jesus:
> Ephesians 2:6

In this way the bible encourages us to set our affections and mind on things in the heavenly places or things that are above;

> If ye then be risen with Christ,
> Seek those things which are above,
> Where Christ sitteth on the right hand of God

> Set your affection on things above,
> Not on things on the earth.
> Colossians 3:1-2
> (Romans 8:5-8)

See, we are not only raised up by God and made to be seated with Christ Jesus in the heavenly places as joint heirs in his glory; but our sharing in his glory or being glorified together with him is also foundered on how we suffer with him. And this kind of suffering is not because of sin; this kind of suffering is because of the things and situations we might encounter, endure and go through to overcome for the sake of his name (Matthew 10:22; John 15:21), for the sake of his righteousness (2Corinthians 5:21; Matthew 5:10; 1Peter 3:13-14) and for the sake of our faith in him (James 1:2-3; 1Peter 1:6-7).

Surely, if we are to manifest life from the position of where he is, which is his will for us and to share in all that he has in his glory; then we should also know and understand how to experience this kind of suffering in order to be glorified with him. This is because we are glorified in him to also suffer together with him (Romans 8:30; John 17:22; Philippians 1:29; Hebrews 2:10).

For some detailed study on this kind of suffering you can take a look at the following scriptures:

John 1:12; Philippians 1:29; 1Peter 4:12-16; Philippians 3:10; Acts 5:41; Matthew 5:11-12; 1Peter 4:19; Ephesians 2:10; 1Peter 2:20-23

CHAPTER SIX

BEYOND THE CROSS

••••••••••••••••••••

> Giving thanks unto the Father,
> Which hath made us meet to be partakers
> Of the inheritance of the saints in light:
> Who hath delivered us from the power of
> Darkness, and hath translated us into
> The kingdom of his dear Son:
> Colossians 1:12-13

> But ye are a chosen generation,
> A royal priesthood, an holy nation, a peculiar people;
> That ye should shew forth the praises of him
> Who hath called you out of darkness
> Into his marvellous light:
> 1Peter 2:9

ONCE WE WERE DARKNESS, abiding in darkness, being ruled and reigned over by the power of darkness. Those were the times we were outside of Christ Jesus and didn't have any relationship with God. However, the truth of God's word reveals that we are no more under the power of darkness (1John 2:8-10). We have been translated or transferred from our original place of sin and darkness into a new place or kingdom of light by God. We are no more darkness but light (Ephesians 5:8; 1Thessalonians 5:5; Matthew 5:14). We are no more in the darkness but in the light from where we can arise and shine for the glory of God upon our lives to be seen (Colossians 1:12; 1John

2:10; Isaiah 60:1-2; John 17:22; 1John 1:7) and therefore no more ruled over by the power of darkness and sin but by the power of light (1John 1:5).

Neither are we the same old persons as we used to be. This divine translation or transfer affected every area of our being; spiritually, physically, mentally and emotionally. It even affects our financial and material positions where seeking the welfare of our new place and position of the kingdom in which we are becomes a priority (Matthew 6:33) and where our source of prosperity becomes dependent upon the kingdom of God (2Corinthians 3:5; Deuteronomy 8:18)

From before the cross, through the cross to beyond the cross, we can realize that our Lord and Saviour Jesus Christ went through stages of suffering before entering in his glory. For the Father, this was necessary for us to be able to also enter and share his glory with the beloved Son as the bible says;

> For it became him, for whom
> Are all things, and by whom are all things,
> In bringing many sons unto glory, to make the
> Captain of their salvation perfect through sufferings
> Hebrews 2:10

It should be understood that all things before the cross are in darkness and under the power of darkness. On the other hand, all things that have been translated or transferred through the cross to beyond the cross are in the light and under the power of light. It is therefore in the new and present position, that we as the new creation in Christ abide and live our lives independent of the original old place and position. This divine translation or transfer took place through the cross by the works of Christ Jesus and his shed blood on it.

This divine translation or transfer did not leave us before the cross or at the cross. This divine transfer or translation has actually taken us from before the cross, past the cross and placed or positioned us beyond the cross in the kingdom of his dear Son. We are now in the kingdom of his dear Son. Here, we abide in him and share with him as joint-heirs of all what is in the fullness of God's glory. We now no longer look up to the cross from before us anymore. We now look up to the cross from behind us to see and remember the works that took place on it by Christ to understand from where we have come, where are presently in Christ as new creations and where God's destiny is for us in Christ.

Now, having been divinely translated or transferred into his kingdom also means that we have come to be where he is in his glory in the heavenly places (Ephesians 2:6). This is equally important for us as believers to learn how to behold his glory and to share in his glory (John 17:24; 2Corinthians 3:18; John 1:14; Romans 8:16-19; Luke 9:25-26).

Based on these revelation truths, we should learn how to always envision ourselves by faith in the resurrected and the glorified Christ who is no more as he went to the cross, neither as the Christ who hanged on the cross but as the resurrected Christ beyond the cross in his glory.

It is beyond the cross, after his resurrection and ascension into heaven that we see Christ Jesus who has entered into his glory and is glorified...

> Then he said unto them,
> O fools, and slow of heart to believe
> All that the prophets have spoken: Ought not
> Christ to have suffered these things, and
> To enter into his glory?
> Luke 24:25-26

It is beyond the cross, after his resurrection and ascension into heaven that we see Christ Jesus who has entered into the heavenly places and seated on the Father's right hand...

> So then after the Lord had spoken unto them,
> He was received up into heaven, and sat
> On the right hand of God
> Mark 16:19

> For Christ is not entered
> Into the holy places made with hands,
> Which are the figures of the true;
> But into heaven itself, now to appear
> In the presence of God for us:
> Hebrews 9:24

It is there beyond the cross in the heavenly places on the Father's right hand side that we see our Lord Jesus Christ crowned in glory with all power and authority in his hands…

> And Jesus came and spake unto them,
> Saying, All power is given unto me
> In heaven and in earth
> Matthew 28:18

It is there beyond the cross, crowned in glory that we see Christ Jesus glorified with a name that is above every name, (tribe, tongue and nation); in heaven, on earth and under the earth…

> And being found in fashion as a man,
> He humbled himself, and became obedient unto death,
> Even the death of the cross. Wherefore God also
> Hath highly exalted him, and given him
> A name which is above every name:
> Philippians 2:8-9

With his name exalted above every name, the Lord now gives us the power and the authority to use his name as a means to reign and rule with him in victory over all and everything which he has already nailed onto the cross John 14:13-14; Mark 16:17).

Every works of the flesh was carried by him and nailed to the cross. The curses of sin (poverty, lack and leanness; sicknesses, diseases and even death) were all carried by him and nailed onto the cross (Isaiah 53:4-5; 1Peter 2:24; Matthew 8:17; 1Peter 2:24; Hebrews 9:28).

It is there beyond the cross in the heavenly places on the Father's right hand side that we see Christ Jesus crowned in his glory as head of his Church...

> And hath put all things under his feet,
> And gave him to be the head over all things
> To the church, which is his body, the fullness
> Of him that filleth all in all.
> Ephesians 1:22-23

It is there beyond the cross in the heavenly places on the Father's right hand side that we see our Lord Jesus Christ in his crowned position interceding for us...

> Who is he that condemneth?
> It is Christ that died, yea rather, that is risen again,
> Who is even at the right hand of God, who also
> Maketh intercession for us
> Romans 8:34
> (Hebrews 7:25; 1John 2:1; Romans 8:27)

It is there beyond the cross in the heavenly places on the Father's right hand that we see all the promises of God for us in heaven established in him. It is there also that all the promises of God are made yes and Amen in him...

> For all the promises of God In him
> Are yea, and in him Amen,
> Unto the glory of God by us
> 2Corinthians 1:20

> Let us hold fast the profession of our faith
> Without wavering;
> (For he is faithful that promised)
> Hebrews 10:23

It is also there beyond the cross in the heavenly places on the Father's right hand that we see all our spiritual blessings in the heavenly places established in the glorified Christ Jesus…

> Blessed be the God and Father
> Of our Lord Jesus Christ, who hath blessed us
> With all spiritual blessings in heavenly places in Christ:
> Ephesians 1:3

It is good to know and believe that beyond the cross is the place and position of power and authority for the believer in the glorified Christ Jesus.

There beyond the cross is the realm of eternity. There is where eternal life is lived and the resurrection power experienced through a life of righteousness and holiness. Beyond the cross is the place and position of the born again believer in Christ. Beyond the cross is the place and position for the new creation to be where Christ is. It is in this place where Christ is that Christ also can be put on (Ephesians 4:24) and be manifested in and through the believer.

You see, the believer and the new creation in Christ should learn to always believe, see and identify himself to be beyond the cross. When the believer in Christ can envision himself or herself in Christ as not being before the cross and at the cross but beyond the cross, it becomes easier for him to release and exercise his faith to receive of God and from God out of the glory in and through Christ (Philippians 4:19; John 14:13-14).

Beyond the cross is the realm of God's glory into which we are called of God by Christ…

> But the God of all grace,
> Who hath called us unto his eternal
> Glory by Christ Jesus, after that ye have suffered
> A while, make you perfect, stablish, strengthen, settle you.
> 1Peter 5:10

> That ye would walk worthy of God,

Who hath called you unto his kingdom and glory
1 Thessalonians 2:12

Beyond the cross is the realm of the supernatural where signs, wonders and miracles are… Beyond the cross is the realm of salvation, healing and deliverance.

Beyond the cross is the divine liberty by which Christ has set us free; and the word of God declares that if the Son shall set you free; brother, sister and beloved in Christ, you are free in deed. Believe to enjoy your freedom and liberty in him beyond the cross as you meditate on the following scriptures.

If the Son therefore shall make you free,
Ye shall be free indeed.
John 8:36

Stand fast therefore in the liberty
Wherewith Christ hath made us free, and
Be not entangled again with the yoke of bondage.
Galatians 5:1

As free, and not using your liberty
For a cloke of maliciousness, but as
The servants of God
1Peter 2:16

For, brethren, ye have been called
Unto liberty; only use not liberty for an occasion
To the flesh, but by love serve one another.
Galatians 5:13

IN CONCLUSION…

But ye are come unto mount Sion,
And unto the city of the living God, the heavenly Jerusalem,

> And to an innumerable company of angels, to the general
> Assembly and church of the firstborn, which are
> written in heaven,
> And to God the Judge of all and to the spirits of just men
> made perfect,
> And to Jesus the mediator of the new covenant,
> and to the blood
> Of sprinkling, that speaketh better things than that of Abel.
> Hebrews 12:22-24

What is important with the message in this book is not just the knowledge being passed on. Rather, it is the revelation of the transfer that has taken place in the life of the believer through the cross of Christ and how he can muster the faith to believe and identify with it to experience the true life in the resurrected and glorified Christ beyond the cross.

It is for the believer in Christ to know where he stands through this transfer or translation as a new creation and the resurrection power that invested in him through the works of Christ and his shed blood on it.

Moreover, it is for the Christian to know and understand how that through the cross of Christ, the believer in Christ has been delivered, made free indeed and set at liberty to enjoy the fullness of life in Christ and the glory into which he has been called.

We are no more in the darkness before the cross. We have been translated from darkness through the cross of Christ into God's marvelous light beyond the cross where all the fullness of God for us in Christ is located. And that being in Christ, we have come to the place of light to rise up in the glory of God upon our lives.

> But ye are a chosen generation,
> A royal priesthood, an holy nation, a peculiar people;
> That ye should shew forth the praises of him who hath
> Called you out of darkness into his marvellous light:
> Which in time past were not a people, but are

Now the people of God: which had not obtained
Mercy, but now have obtained mercy.
1Peter 2:9-10

Arise, shine; for thy light is come,
And the glory of the Lord is risen upon thee.
For, behold, the darkness shall cover the earth,
And gross darkness the people:
But the Lord shall arise upon thee,
And his glory shall be seen upon thee.
Isaiah 60:1-2

To God be the glory

www.ingramcontent.com/pod-product-compliance
Lightning Source LLC
Chambersburg PA
CBHW021154080526
44588CB00008B/326